COMPASS FOR
INTERCULTURAL PARTNERSHIPS

CW01425507

LIVINGstone
centre of competence for
intercultural entrepreneurship

About Living Stone Centre

Inspiration and expertise have laid the foundations of The Living Stone Centre of Competence for Intercultural Entrepreneurship. Its mission statement is to deploy the integration of cultures as a source of welfare and tolerance in a glocalising world. Together with K.U. Leuven, Joker Tourism and Cera, the Centre adds the concept of 'interculturality' to tomorrow's entrepreneurship, in profit and non-profit sectors.

www.lscoop.com

Compass for Intercultural Partnerships

*A thought provoking book to deploy the integration
of cultures as a source of welfare and tolerance
in a glocalising world*

BOB ELSEN, IGNACE POLLET, PATRICK DEVELTERE
Introduction by KOENRAAD DEBACKERE

Leuven University Press
2007

© 2007 by Leuven University Press / Presses Universitaires de Louvain /
Universitaire Pers Leuven
Minderbroedersstraat 4, B-3000 Leuven (Belgium)

ISBN 978 90 5867 607 8

D / 2007 / 1869 / 27
NUR: 763

Cover: Jurgen Leemans

INTERCULTURALISM NEEDS
A COMPASS INDEED ...

European society is currently confronted with tremendous intercultural challenges, both at home and in its relationships with the many members of an increasingly global world. The nature and the sustainability of socio-economical and political relationships between the multitude of cultures all over the globe therefore deserves our close attention. This focus calls for macro-level policies and actions. They are, however, important and necessary but not sufficient. Indeed, any macro-level policy on intercultural relationships that wants to be successful, should be underpinned and supported by a variety of micro-level strategies and actions. These micro-level strategies and actions do necessitate a deep understanding of interculturalism at the level of individual actors and their organizations. These relationships between individuals should be embedded in a context of trust and mutual understanding. This is definitely true for all of us who want to stimulate wealth creation through intercultural entrepreneurship and economic development. The creation of Living Stone Cooperation is an innovative attempt to fill the gap between macro-level policy making and micro-level actions in the day-to-day reality of intercultural entrepreneurship.

The combination of interculturalism and entrepreneurship has proved to be a very attractive and challenging one for all the founders involved, not at least for K.U.Leuven. K.U.Leuven indeed has developed a coherent and consistent policy to foster and to stimulate entrepreneurship amongst its faculty. This has led to the creation and the growth of Leuven R&D, the technology transfer office of K.U.Leuven. Since the mid-eighties up to the first quarter of 2007, Leuven R&D has been at the origin of 73 entrepreneurial spin-off companies. These companies are active across a broad range of technical and economic sectors. Their existence and their successful development has fostered the reputation of Leuven R&D as one of the major generators of academic spin-offs in Europe. The creation of Leuven.Inc, in 1999, further illustrates the emphasis of K.U.Leuven on entrepreneurial activity. Leuven.Inc started as a network organization with an ambition to bring together like-minded people driving the genesis and growth of new business activity in the Leuven area. Today Leuvin.Inc is thriving, with a population of 600 active members who form the cornerstone of academic entrepreneurship in the region.

At the same time, K.U.Leuven research and education is steeped in a tradition of intercultural understanding and cooperation. Various faculty research groups have been active in this area. Their focus has ranged from social to economical over political issues. They have generated widespread interest and recognition on the basis of their research programs. HIVA, a buoyant research institute at K.U.Leuven, has been active in the field of intercultural policy and development for many years. The institute has attained an internationally visible and renowned position in the world of intercultural cooperation and development, not to the least thanks to the ever-lasting vision and efforts of its director, Professor Patrick Develtere.

As a consequence, it was a novel but also logical step to combine the strengths of HIVA and Leuven R&D into a major new initiative on intercultural entrepreneurship. The opportunity to do so arose when Bob Elsen, an entrepreneur himself as well as an alumnus of K.U.Leuven, introduced a proposal to start both a research-oriented and an application-oriented collaboration on the topic of intercultural entrepreneurship. Being the "founding father" of Joker Toerisme, a successful company that attempts to bridge the cultural distance between people through travel and exploration, as well as the ViaVia travel cafés, he disposes of an ideal network of relationships and a rich portfolio of insights that, coupled to the K.U.Leuven tradition of entrepreneurship practice and research on interculturalism, inevitably should lead to a win-win project. Thus the Living Stone project was born. In order to stress the dual aim of this project, we created both Living Stone Cooperation (LSC), a non-for-profit company that will support entrepreneurial projects in various countries all over the globe, and Living Stone Fund (LSF), a research chair at K.U.Leuven that will enlarge and deepen our understanding of intercultural entrepreneurship. By having a non-for-profit organization linked with a research chair, the founders of the Living Stone initiative do hope that they will be able to approach the topic in a novel, much more integrated way than has been the case before. The combination of LSC and LSF therefore is an innovation in and of itself. It combines theory and application in a highly tangible and practical manner.

7

This book is the result of the first two years of our joint endeavors. The various topics covered illustrate the path we have followed sofar and the fruits we have harvested. Our activity portfolio has grown and can rightly be coined impressive, thanks to the joint efforts of the various share-holders and stakeholders involved in LSC and LSF. Professor Develtere has brought his rich and varied insights on cooperative intercultural activity to the table, as the reader will enjoy to see and read. The experiences developed with Joker and ViaVia have led to the creation of a portfolio of activities "in the field," ranging from special travel arrange-ments to dedicated projects over specific local education and training programs. The development of the insightful "coconut model" underpins these experiences. The reader will be charmed by it. Finally, since the start of our opera-tions, we had the pleasure to welcome two new stakehold-ers: Cera Foundation and KBC Group. Cera Foundation also became a shareholder in LSC. By joining LSC, both partners stress their vivid commitment to the ambitions and aims set by the initial founders of both LSC and LSF. It is a right and just cause. We will sustain it and cherish it with the best of efforts we can spend. Furthermore, the spillovers to a better understanding of interculturalism within Flem-ish society, will be a nice additional effect all along the path we jointly create and walk.

May 'LSC' and 'LSF' continue their road to success!

Prof. Dr. Ir. Koenraad Debackere
Chairman Living Stone Cooperation

CONTENTS

The World
in a Coconut

*A personal view
to inspire*

BOB ELSEN

The world in a coconut

IN DIVERSITY THERE IS STRENGTH

Cultural diversity has never before been so strongly present in the world as it is today. It has become an essential element of our society both in our professional and private life.

Cultural interactions, whether they enhance or reduce each other, are on the increase as a result of globalisation. Such crossing of cultures results inevitably into new mentalities and interactions, which in turn lead to new concepts and realisations.

One such realisation is the Living Stone Centre of Competence (LSC)[1] for Intercultural Entrepreneurship, founded in 2005 by the Catholic University of Leuven (Katholieke Universiteit Leuven, K.U.Leuven) and Joker Tourism (Joker Toerisme). The LSC is a partnership with social objectives and its mission is to deploy the integration of cultures as a source of welfare and tolerance in a 'glocalising'[2] world.

The first part of this article, entitled 'And remember, no matter where you go, there you are', concentrates on some thoughts that inspired and urged the founders of the centre to give interculturality its own undisputed place in the agenda of the enterprising of the glocalised world. The section 'Cultural Sensitivity' introduces the concepts of culture and interculturality, explains the coconut model developed by the LSC and presents the intercultural sensitivity training offered.

It must be noted that all developments presented here were made possible thanks to the driving force of many spiritual colleagues, whom I warmly thank.

The LSC is a manifestation of the modern saying "in diversity there is strength", being a dynamic cross-breed of two cultures: that of Leuven University, with its expertise in scientific research, and that of Joker Toerisme nv with the strength of 25 years of experience in sustainable tourism and enterprise. Mutual sharing of knowledge, know-how and resources significantly enhances not only the Centre's competitiveness on a national and international level but strengthens the individual parties in their own activities.

The Centre is a non-profit cooperation that fosters an awareness and appreciation of cultural difference. Valuing diversity is no longer merely a social goal that we teach our children in the family and in schools. It has become the goal of any employer as the make-up of the work force changes rapidly, with most companies and organisations now being collectives of individuals from diverse groups. Learning how to communicate effectively with one another and how to reach mutual understandings helps to prevent misunderstandings, and their associated failures, and leads to motivation and success.

The LSC prepares its customers whether entrepreneurs, development workers, local business partners or travellers for the impact with other cultures. Such cultural contact is no longer confrontational but truly rewarding and teaches

14

the participants how to be with other cultures without feeling either threatened by the others or seeing themselves as stereotypes of their own culture. Our customers develop insights and skills through the exploration of and integration with various cultures. They experience that 'being different' is a rich source for innovation and development and not an obstacle for success.

The LSC teaches companies and organisations how to incorporate cultural insight and understanding successfully in their development of international operations strategies.

It concentrates on how people of different cultural background correlate to one another and how the global and the local can strengthen each other. Although the mentalities in the four corners of the earth will never be the same, there is no doubt that interactions between cultures have made the world not only a more colourful place in which to live and operate, but at the same time a more challenging one. It is an evolutionary fact: survival largely depends on a fast response to any changes in the surroundings. The tougher the terrain, the faster must be the change, if extinction is to be avoided. The entrepreneurial world is undoubtedly a tough terrain and survival in it requires not only alertness and active contact with the surroundings but foresight and preparation for each eventuality. After all, "Gouverner, c'est prévoir"[3].

Just a Tip

1. In a blender, add coconut milk with one quarter Cachaça (a Brazilian sugar cane liqueur), a big dash of rum, a smaller dash of double cream and two ice cubes.
2. Shake well, pour into a glass of your choice.
3. Sit comfortably, take a sip and start with the article... Guaranteed for an agreeable read.

AND REMEMBER, NO MATTER WHERE YOU GO,
THERE YOU ARE.
(Confucius)

Twenty years ago, I came for the first time to Mali to develop a new destination for Joker. Over centuries, Mali grew along the river Niger relishing many impressive kingdoms and cities like Djenné and Timbuktu. However, during the colonial period, the Sahel[4], once among the most developed regions of black Africa, degraded to a source for labour for the colonial economy of Senegal. In the period that followed Mali degenerated to one of the poorest countries in the world.

Discovering the Dogon Bandiagara Escarpment in the Mopti region, with around three hundred villages scattered along the sandstone cliffs, was a complete surprise to me. The villages had remained unchanged for 500 years. The French travel guide "Guide du Routard" was limiting itself to walks of two, three and four hours. We walked for seven entire days. Our food and drink being carried for us – apart from onions, a chicken or goat we could not buy anything else – and the native staple food was the same for breakfast, lunch and supper: the sticky *tô*[5]. Sleeping under the roof of the *'chef du village'* – there was no other tourist accommodation outside the camp in Sangha. Waking up at day break only to find thirty or forty women lined up with their sick children – white men were considered to be doctors and there was only one health centre for the three hundred villages. Washing ourselves, four of us, in one bucket of water – for the women of Dogon, a bucket of water meant a forty minute walk to the well along slippery stony paths up and down the cliffs. Children would run away, startled to see us, women would approach to touch our skin to make sure that there was no other colour underneath it. Except for the radio connection in the bigger village of Sangha, there was no other means of modern communication. During the seven-day hike we came across no other tourists.

I found Mali to be a colourful melting pot of peoples and, despite the poverty, some things stood out: the music, the scents, the colours and above all the dignity of its people. After all this is timeless Africa. And I am not sure what it was. Perhaps it was the good-humoured villagers, the hustle and bustle of their hamlets, the raw beauty of everything around me. Maybe it was just the intense colours or the light. Whatever it was there is no doubt in my mind. Mali was not only a fascinating discovery. Mali had strengthened my soul.

I have been back many times since. Now there are dams and many water wells which make the work for women much easier. Scattered here and there like a green patchwork pattern on a stone desert are allotments for tomatoes, cabbage, lettuce, mangos and herbs, apart from the humble onions. Medical care and education are beginning to improve. There are mobile phones and internet, and Nike has the same value as a symbol here as it has in western countries. Tourism is definitely developed as many visitors are drawn to this impressive area. There are hotels and souvenir shops in every village. As a consequence the young generation no longer needs to go to Bamako and elsewhere to make a living, but stays here.

The world of the Mali people has undoubtedly been changed radically and is still changing, sometimes unexpectedly so, and to the point of non-recognition. The new generations find themselves unavoidably in a bigger entity. Not without downfalls: cheaper foreign imports of textiles, motorbikes, tools and appliances have destroyed the native production. Between 1997 and 2002 Mali suffered losses of US$30 million per year of export revenue as a result of subsidized cotton crops in developed countries[6]. Here, globalisation, is not a superfluous luxury. It is a fact of everyday life.

Perhaps the possession of knowledge, that used to belong to the "elders", is now acquired through contact and internet by the young generation. Perhaps now Malians listen to jazz and drink Cola. But the wooden masks, which the locals believe to hold power, are kept away from the tourists. Instead imitations are used during the dances staged for the visitors. Being part of the world does not mean abandoning what natives still hold sacred or forgetting who you really are.

Offspring of Time

Not only Mali has changed. The world itself is changing. In Ayacucho (Peru) mothers walk around in their wide skirts with an old-fashioned bowler-like hat on their heads next to their daughters in jeans and with belly piercing. In

Dakar (Senegal) and in other big African cities the number of births is limited following the western model and the care of the elderly is passed on more and more to the state. In Shanghai (China) the young girls do not exchange readily their freedom for marriage. And everywhere one wears the same T-shirts and Nikes, drinks Cola and Nescafé, and watches "Friends" and "Desperate Housewives".

It cannot be denied that as a result of globalisation a predominantly American cultural model functions as an example world wide. But how deep is its influence? Is it a commercial one, limiting itself into the 'cultural hardware' like technology and clothes fashion, or does it extend its tentacles much deeper, into the 'cultural software' like ideals and values?

For cultures are built out of two elements: the legacy of the past which truly defines a culture and is based on values and norms of ancestors, traditions and religion; and the other one that 'develops now' arising from current influences, world wide interactions, information influx, intertwining economies and blending of cultures. It is this latter element that greatly determines the direction of the evolution of a culture and in this sense the children become the offspring of their time and less son of their fathers.

Cultures are dynamic and increasingly they will blend more. The uptake of elements from other cultures is a logical occurrence. It will become a positive process as long as people can retain their dignity. If these days we tend to put much more emphasis on our diversities, it is because we are becoming more and more homogenised. Globalisation has only two alternatives: diversity where the right to be an individual is respected, or uniformity, where any alternative thinking is wrong. Until recently the extinction of cultures received less attention than the extinction of animal and plant species. Yet uniformity is barrenness, diversity is enrichment: "Le plaisir de découvrir la différence de l'autre"[7]. And cultural diversity has to prevail as there is an inherent need in humans for differentiated identity.

Basic ingredients...

Culture
But what really is culture? A matter-of-fact definition holds culture to be a human creation, either shared or imposed, and passed on to the next generations through customs and traditions. It provides us with a framework within which we define our identity and develop our attitudes, values and behaviour. Any subsequent interaction we have with the others is an interpretation and an extrapolation of our cultural identity. In this manner culture interferes with everything in our life, from the mundane to the spiritual. That makes Homo Sapiens more than a bunch of flesh and bones.

Culture is hence not only the specific way in which a group of people live their life but also the particular way in which the group regards the others and their respective world. And as such, culture is for man what water is to fish. Take it away and the effects are disastrous.

21

... for a potent cocktail.

Interculturality

The interaction, exchange and communication between people of different cultures is interculturality. Interculturality is the cross-pollination between North and South, East and West and as such it is an outstanding model of integration as the individual recognises and accepts the reciprocity of the culture of the others. Interculturality strives for a pluralistic transformation of societies whereby the boundaries between cultures are in constant motion or become indistinct. Institutions, companies and organisations will find that for successful realisation of their goals, integration of culture becomes a factor more important than the management of diversity. Cultural diversity may enrich the social fabric of life but it is interculturality which will make a difference in the undertaking of the future, just like creativity and innovation are doing at present.

Multiculturality and interculturality are often used, and erroneously so, interchangeably. They are two separate terms which define cultural diversity.

Multiculturality: The earlier model of 'bend or break', with dominant and subordinate cultures, has been replaced by the 'multicultural' model which recognises cultural differences and respects cultural entities. The new model strives for a harmonious co-existence between the established and the subsequently introduced culture, retaining, however, the differences between them. A transition into a more just society is expressed in the well-known 'Equal Opportunities' policy. Such a policy aims at the protection of the weakest members by introducing rules for positive discrimination of socially disadvantaged or minority groups.

Interculturality: A step further than multiculturality, cultures are encouraged to interact and blend or fuse. It focuses primarily on the added value created for each culture through such interactions. Contrary to what some believe, interculturality does not remove authenticity: the Masai warriors may watch television and use the internet. Their way of life and hence the culture that they will pass on to the next generation has radically been changed but nevertheless they carry their mobile phone still next to their traditional spear! Interculturality acts just like a kaleidoscope where different elements are brought together: light, colour and shapes combine into a perfect image for one single moment out of all eternity with each turn of the tube. The result, different each time, is always surprising and wonderful.

Dynamic or Dynamite?

Diversity of Cultural Identity and its Challenges
There are various forms of culture: from the dominant (national culture, for example) to the subordinate (familial, religious cultures, company cultures, organisational cultures). Any interactions between these forms, although with immense advantages, have potential pitfalls. The reason is that any contact with new worlds of diverse thinking and behav-

iour patterns often leaves us, as outsiders, with the feeling that such worlds possess an elusive nature. Each such contact removes us from our own frame of reference and places us in direct confrontation with a different perception of the world. One example: the world can be viewed as a *Gestalt*[8] or as a field experience[9]. As Gestalt: the senses record images that are configured into structures who are concrete and easily communicable. As field: think about a magnetic field which cannot be perceived by the senses but only by its actions – magnets attracting nails. In the same manner a person experiences things from his environmental field through perception supplemented by reflection and emotions. These field experiences are also a reality. Compare the formal description of a painting in a catalogue with the impressions that that same painting may provoke. Commonly Gestalt is more related to the West creating a breeding ground for sciences and technology; field experience is more attributed to the East valuing mysticism and aesthetics.

Cultural conflicts are, perhaps, avoidable. Yet they do not arise through cultural differences but rather through ignorance about others, and hence erroneous interpretation of attitudes and behaviour patterns different to our own. In some Asiatic and Arab countries touching with the left hand is seen as offensive, as that hand is regarded inferior to the right one. Different views of time are fostered by different cultures: the Malian think, "Vous avez l'horloge, nous avons le temps"[10], for Indonesians "time is elastic like rubber", and then there is the Spanish 'mañana'[11] in the sense that there is still time tomorrow. These may be just a handful of examples that raise a smile or two when recited, but then there are much more serious ones concerning religion, values regarding life, women, money and so on.

Most conflicts, and sadly those of a more serious nature, arise through a feeling of superiority, or what I term here the 'We syndrome'. Take for example the consideration by the West of the western entrepreneurial culture, social security and democracy as the examples to be followed without ever questioning them, or placing them in another culture and in a different historical or socio-economic context. Or the belief that the centre of the world was, is and shall remain in the next thousand years, always in 'our' West. These are being proved counterproductive, as nowadays world wide there is a transition from ideology to cultural identity, a return to deeply rooted cultural values and beliefs, which is often seen as a reaction to such western beliefs and economic domination, and it often has religion as its determining factor. In its extreme form this transition expresses itself in fundamentalist moves which divide the world into 'us, the good ones' and 'them, the bad ones'.

The football war in 1969 between El Salvador and Honduras serves as a disturbing reminder of what can go wrong when the 'We syndrome' operates. The war lasted six days with a death toll of 2000 because of differences in the colour of their scarves, irrespective of the strong similarities between victims and offenders. The syndrome also fuels sporadic incidents involving skin colour or ethnic group with disastrous results when it is consciously manipulated into fear. We fear what we do not know. And we hate what we fear. And fear leads to murder: if I do not strike first I leave the chance to the opposition not only to kill myself but also my family and friends. Then the 'We syndrome' culminates in organised hooliganism and worse so, in genocide all around the world.

It would be better if everyone were encouraged to consider one's cultural identity as a sum of influences from different origins which evolve all the time and render cultural identities a dynamic nature. Just like reality. The mixture of elements that form a cultural identity, originates from a blend of one's own culture with other dominant and subordinate cultures. Just like a Szechuan is also a Chinese, I am at the same time Flemish (area Flanders), Belgian, and to go a step further I am European influenced by Japanese Zen, Mali's griots[12] and Argentinean tango, loving Honduras Rum, French wine and world-wide Coca-Cola.

Not only does culture define our attitudes, values and behaviour, but also the manner in which we regard others. By defining or interpreting this, we find out what is cultural identity and how it intervenes in every day life. It is this interpretation from one's own culture that is also a fundamental aspect of any subsequent cultural cross-breeding. Intolerance occurs whenever the identity of a person is defined from one origin, and one hardly ever places one's self in another person's shoes or attempts to hold a dialogue. There are two requirements for a breeding ground of tolerance: the first is the realisation and acceptance of one's cultural diversity – in other words identifying one's self with one's colourful culture placed in today's world. The second is that the various cultures must remain open for one another while they place and integrate themselves in a universal world retaining their individual dynamic value.

Multinational enterprises build their own identity just like individuals. Integration and blending of own, dominant and subordinate cultures are also essential here for better functioning. And conflicts have to be prevented.

Now we really need a compass

It is a common sight in Buenos Aires even today: elderly men searching in rubbish bins. One gets used to it. After all it is such occurrences that traditionally define 'the South'. Yet in 2006 I found the same sight in my hometown Leuven extremely disturbing and hard to accept. Insignificant? A mere sentimental personal observation? Perhaps not when Indian companies are buying up Belgian ones while Belgian NGO funds are deployed for vital development projects, like those of sister Jeanne Devos[13] in Mumbai, or of WIN[14] in Calcutta, in the very same India. Today the same cultural, social, economic, religious and political layers are present all over the world. 'The South' is now located also in the North, West and East and vice versa. The definition of 'North' and 'South' has long been shaken to its roots. And as the visual distinction between North and South, East and West disappear, one definitely

27

needs the old compass. At least it still points to magnetic North. For the moment.

Globalisation, increased mobility, knowledge and information exchanges result in higher migration of people. This has its repercussions on the entrepreneurial world and not only on its work force. Organisations and enterprises deal increasingly more and more with other, far-away countries and such a phenomenon is certainly not a one-way movement; India and China invest around the world. The growing poles in Asia become engines that shake the West and conquer the western markets, raising enormous volumes of international purchasing power. In 2006 their export surplus against US and EU was estimated at 400 billion dollars[15]. This launches world wide a geopolitical leverage: conquest of imported raw materials, the buying of companies in the West, the impact on Eurasia, Africa and Latin America. How many people reflect on the fact that China supports the deficient trade balance of the US? In the meantime the other giant, India, works in between with its self-willed way further into its globalisation.

Not being able to look further than the end of one's nose is neither a contemporary characteristic nor a western privilege. History is scattered with examples of empires and kingdoms which fell into decay throughout the world. Organisations and enterprises are no different and many have faced serious problems for the very same reason.

The statements "my village is the world" and "the world is my village" have long lost their traditional literal meaning. Yet our way of thinking is trailing behind as we are still locked in the old interpretation. Prejudices and stereotypes including those concerning appearances undermine our view of the world everywhere: the English follow the rules but they are bad chefs, the French wear berets, are unfriendly but excellent chefs, all Germans are efficient but have no sense of humour while the Americans are all fat and rich.[16] Stereotypes are definitely a harmless source of jokes:

> In a perfect world, the chefs would all be French, the police British and the mechanics German. But imagine life if chefs were British, mechanics were French and cops were German ...

Alexander the Great, the famous Macedonian leader of antiquity, may have been suffering from erratic, destructive behaviour but he was certainly great, even if it were for one thing alone. His is perhaps the first recorded case of applied sensitivity for cultures. At some stage in his campaign in the Persian empire in the years 330-327BC, Alexander realised that conquering the world was not enough. One had also to rule it with no conflicts. He made concessions to the native population by showing respect for their customs, he appointed natives to important positions, dressed himself according to the local customs and he reverted to marrying his generals to local women. He himself married Roxane, a local princess from the Sogdian region. I do not mean to imply that businesses operating in foreign countries should include in their relocation packages a local wedding, but it is food for thought!

Ralph Emerson[17] once wrote that the secret of life is conversation and the greatest success is confidence. Nothing could be more true and these two secrets are the basis for the development of cultural awareness and intercultural sensitivity. One can only find about other cultures through dialogue and such findings strengthen one's own confidence for their own cultural identity. Real contact with cultural diversity requires an open mind, shedding of stereotypes, abandoning traditional certainties. Only then can integration of new elements and the broadening of any frame of reference be

THE WORLD IN A COCONUT

possible. Seeing other cultures as they really are enhances our insight into our own cultural identity, and it does not mean accepting or agreeing with what they have to offer.

No Pain No Gain

Development of cultural competence and its various components, like cultural sensitivity, does not occur in brief workshops and classes. It is an individual, active life-long process of learning and practising. There are several distinct grades in any personal contact with other cultures and they vary from culture to culture. For example one may be more absorbed in the Argentinean than the Brazilian culture though equally fascinated by both. It all depends on the attitude of the person involved, their knowledge and affinity, their imagination and their experience with the culture in question. In the 80's and 90's there was an attempt to move beyond discrimination issues to a real ability to work appropriately with cultural difference. It was realised that this was a planned sequence of development and a framework was created to describe the reactions of people to cultural differences. Such a framework can further be used for determining how to work and improve the capacity for intercultural sensitivity and collaboration. The development runs into a number of stages, different for each person. The stages presented here are a modification of the stages in original model created by Milton Bennett in 1986 and 1993 and widely known as DMIS (Developmental Model of Intercultural Sensitivity).

Stages in the development for cultural sensitivity
1. Denial
People in this stage are very unaware of cultural difference. One looks at the world starting from one's own cultural background as a reference point. Whenever one is confronted with another culture one begins to react by:
- Refusal ('only my values, there are no others')
- Dismissal and defensiveness ('only we possess the truth, the rest is wrong and threatening')
- Minimalising (there are differences, but they are insignificant)

2. Taking an interest
In this second stage, cultural differences are perceived but personal motives and environmental factors define the extent of our interest. We are about to observe and open up to cultural differences and similarities. During this phase we consider a culture with interest but still through the lens of our own culture and any differences from ourselves are viewed with reservation.

3. Recognising and Acknowledging
We interpret differences and similarities while we analyse cultural values and behaviour patterns through knowledge of and insight into the different layers of culture. Perception of the world and starting points different to our own, produce different behaviour and values. Understanding and accepting this will enable us to grow in our 'understanding' and appreciation of the others and of ourselves. One learns how to look through the eyes of the others.

4. *Creating a dialogue*

Any increase in the skills for exploring cultures will induce more trust and better communication with the other cultures. Cultural diversity will then be regarded as a potential asset for success and not as an obstacle.

5. *Internalising*

We sharpen up attitudes which focus on better attunement to and integration of cultures. Cultural integration creates new values and insights, broadens mentalities and produces new concepts. Sensitivity towards the 'Intercultural' becomes second nature.

From exploring to integrating, from integrating to exploring

Intercultural sensitivity training

The Living Stone Centre views cultural diversity as a source for new possibilities and not as a cause for imbalance and conflict. This philosophy is successfully applied in the intercultural sensitivity training programs developed by the Centre. The programs prepare the participants for effective and successful co-operation between, and exchange of, cultures by stimulating them to develop intercultural sensitivity. In addition the programs lead the participants to a stronger reflection of their own identity. The awareness of cultural diversity is subsequently deployed in the broadening of mentalities for successful interactions and co-operation and in conflicts resolution. Such a new curriculum adds a missing link to the Corporate Social Responsibility as interculturality is integrated into strategic thinking, equivalent to innovation and creativity.

The programs are aimed at enterprises, companies and organisations, the non-profit sector and government and all those who have the ambition to be enriched and strengthened by their cultural diversity. They deploy mind and heart, rational and emotional intelligence, open-mindedness and require to a large extent sincerity and impartiality. The participants are encouraged to go beyond the mere registering of cultural differences and similarities and to draw more value out of cultural exchange. They learn more successful communication, more effective trading and decision making through conscious observation and enhanced cultural awareness. Results take effect as much on personal level as in the organisational or professional environment within which one functions. Sensitivity to interculturality then becomes second nature.

Developing cultural sensitivity is a life-long process from exploring to integrating, from integrating to exploring ... In reality one moves back and forth between the different stages. On the basis of the general model described above, the distinct stages of exploring and integrating have been further developed in the following cycle (Figure 1):

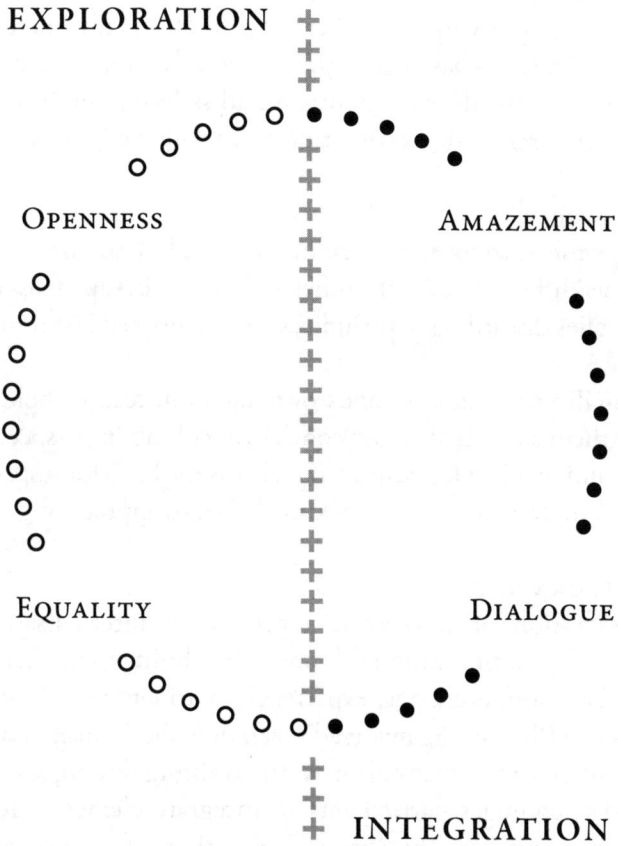

Figure 1. Cycling between Exploring and Integrating

Exploring

Exploring or discovering different cultures is 'active listening and observing' the other culture. This is not merely a technique. It is based on authenticity and extreme attention to detail. The developed insight and skills empower us for better observation, recognition and acknowledgment.

Key concepts:

Openness: to open yourself in the first place to 'the Other' as 'different', to see the other as the other is. Openness implies discarding of prejudices and traditional certainties.

Equality: to question one's own values instead of holding them as evident. It puts one's own culture in perspective and makes it less central. Equality is the basis for respect.

Action: To recognise and acknowledge, to appreciate.

Integrating

Integration of cultures is a process of internalisation. Only by adding rational knowledge (built upon theory, observation, exchange, experience) with emotional intelligence ('becoming involved'), can one obtain insight and sensitivity for other cultures. The training develops skills and encourages participants to integrate elements from various cultures. This 'bringing together' of cultures and ideas, concepts and products creates additional values which become the differentiating factors of success in the enterprise of tomorrow.

Key concepts:

Dialogue: it requires a certain amount of input and works interactively. It is an exchange based on the realisation that all parties involved have something to offer, each one out of their own identity. As a result one's own identity is considerably strengthened.

Action: to exchange, to become involved

Amazement: primordial astonishment remains the fundamental onset to exploration, to deeper reflection. Amazement touches mind and heart. Through this insight, knowledge and innovation grow.

Action: to internalise, to allow one to be inspired.

The training is built around the two poles described above: exploring and integrating and entails a modular part and/ or a hands-on training.

A Traditional Training

The modular part of the training covers the topics of interculturality and introduces the Living Stone Coconut Model. The various modules stimulate the participants to make full use of their personal potential in an environment with no boundaries through the development of cultural awareness and the development of insights and skills in intercultural exploration and in intercultural integration. Knowledge and modification of attitudes are brought about on the basis of theoretical models, case studies, interactive participation with questions and dialogue, and observations based on active listening and field experience.

The modules are tailored to the requirements and the specifications of the company or organisation in individual project packages which are determined by the concrete expectations and demands of the customer.

Living Stone Gateways: A Different Training

The Living Stone Gateways have a different approach to the intercultural preparation. The sensitivity training is processed into intercultural experience trips to the target country. The Gateways are tailored specifically to the participant company or organisation in a limited group of around ten people with interactive experience exchanges. They last for one week with a balance between formal and informal contacts, cultural and culinary experiences and sensitivity training in a specific environment of cultural diversity. Until now the Gateways are offered in five countries of pronounced cultural identity: Mali, Argentina, China, India and Romania. A sixth destination, Belgium, has been recently added, offering the chance to foreign organisations and companies to have the reciprocal experience in Europe. After all the promotional quote 'Brussels, the heart of Europe' must make Belgium the gateway to Europe.

THE COCONUT MODEL

The Living Stone Coconut Model is a 'tool kit', a hands-on model borrowed from Nature as the practical visualisation of the make-up of the cultures of the world across their different layers, and from more than one perspective. It is the detailed representation of the first part of the sensitivity training model, namely the stage of Exploring. This practical model for exploring cultures has managed to integrate theories about interculturality from several disciplines.[18] Why the coconut? Its exotic nature and its durable qualities make it the best visual candidate for our training model. Tropical beaches with swaying palm trees is for many the picture of paradise on earth. The swaying coconut palm is indeed a gift from mother Nature. The tree itself provides food, drink, fibres, roofing material, medicines, oil, wood, fuel and household tools. Coconuts have thick, green skin and can grow to a length of about 30 cm and to a weight of 1.5 kg. The brown coconut, as we know it, is actually the seed of the plant, like the pips of an orange. The white flesh and the coconut milk are the nutritional supplies for the seed. The coconut itself is an example of successful integration in cocktails and sauces. Even neat, it is still tasty!

Just like a culture with its several layers (the upper ones associated with behaviour patterns, forms of interactions and their expressions, and the inner layers, or the nucleus, representing values and beliefs), the model has a justified stratified architecture which renders it an appropriate means for observing, recognising and acknowledging, and facilitates the insight to the constituent cultural elements.

The Coconut model offers a safety net when perceiving, arranging and interpreting the various layers of a culture. It does not represent a hierarchy. One can compare the application of such a model with the 4 P's marketing model. Product, price, place and promotion have no hierarchy over each other and the model can be equally deployed whether for a restaurant, a bank a travel agency or other. The various layers in the Living Stone model are also holistic and of equal importance and they can be applied as a whole to cultures.

The Coconut Model consists of five layers, from the visible one to the concealed and unconscious. Before you push to the inside, you observe first the external layers (skin) and the organisational shapes (pith). These layers are the 'hardware' of the culture, sensitive to influences from the external environment. For example you observe here quickly the impact of globalisation. The stronger brown seed capsule is the symbolic guardian of the gate which you have to cross before gaining access to the 'software' of the culture. These layers require more effort to penetrate as their roots are going deep. In the coconut model these translate to the nutrient supplies of the seed: the soft flesh and the coconut milk. These are respectively the layers of the foundations and the unconscious inherent patterns. This nucleus is not tangible just like each culture is not in its essential form.

Five layers

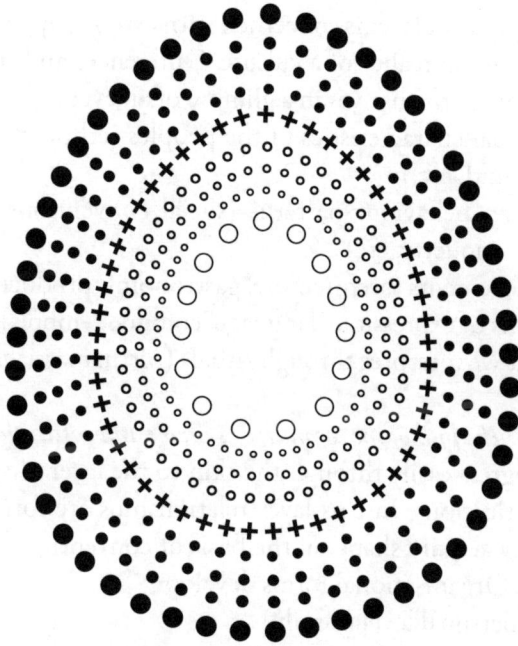

O Universal patterns   ●●● Systems & institutions

○○○ Foundations   ● Outward appearances

+ Dividing the visible
and the hidden

Figure 2. The five layers of the Coconut Model represent culture, from the exterior to the interior. The circular shape aims to draw attention to the nucleus. However the coconut represents also 'wholeness', as everything is linked to everything else.[19]

Layer 5. The coconut skin, or external appearances and visual reality.

The uppermost layer is concerned with external appearances and the visual reality of a culture. Differences and similarities manifest themselves in a glimpse of an eye:

▷ external characteristics of the peoples (ethnicity, physical build, etc.)
▷ human behaviour patterns (social conventions, greetings, etiquette, etc)
▷ achievements (architecture, gastronomy, products, art)
▷ means of expression (language, colours, symbols)
▷ what we interpret through rituals (birth, marriage, etc)

Layer 4. The pith of the coconut, or systems and institutions

We progress easily through the skin to the layer of systems and institutions. In this layer relationships are formalised and they acquire shape on the basis of conventions and attitudes. Organisational forms develop:

▷ at a personal level (family)
▷ in businesses and organisations
▷ at the level of society

Layer 3. The shell of the coconut seed, a symbolic dividing line

The strong brown coconut seed shell symbolises the differentiation between 'the Visible' and 'the Hidden' of cultures. Not only a hard nut to crack but infinitely more difficult to digest. Just like an iceberg, what lies beneath the surface is far greater. These layers are the defining force behind any perceived behaviour. More effort is required for greater insight into a culture.

Layer 2. The flesh of the seed or the foundations
This is where one stumbles upon the foundations of a culture. They are not visible but they do define how people behave. The foundations 'feed' the culture through:
▷ beliefs
▷ norms and values. Both define our ideas about good and evil but norms are often determined externally and imposed via social control, whereas values are more individual in nature.
▷ attitudes and conventions
▷ dealing with emotions
▷ dealing with violence and war

Layer 1. The coconut milk or universal patterns
This inner layer is associated with universal patterns[20], common to each culture: community feeling versus individualism; justice versus injustice; high or low context; status vs skill; rules vs flexibility; impersonal vs emotional; direct vs indirect. It is the least tangible and the most inaccessible layer. It prescribes how we deal with others, with time, with nature and religion leaves its mark here. It is a source for attitudes and assumptions which are transferred within a culture from the time of one's birth and they appear self-evident. Hence against all common sense one considers their place of birth as the centre of the world. Such starting points are often not obvious to others and constant confrontation with different starting points may cause emotional reactions. One feels that the rules that one is used to do not apply to others.

Like Coconut?

Coconuts are all different and yet similar. So are people. Similar in body and spirit. In the course of time we may have grown more and more away from each other but our origins are common. Two examples can simply illustrate this:

> Around 4000 years ago the first Indo-Europeans lived around the Black Sea and the Caspian Sea. They began to move in waves to Iran and India, to Greece, Italy and Spain, to England and France, to Scandinavia, to East Europe and Russia. Wherever they went they integrated with the native tribes. The Indian Vedas, Greek philosophy, the Gylfaginning[21] are all written in kindred languages. In related languages one hears related thoughts. They believed in a pantheon. Gods are Azen in Scandinavia, Asura in Sanscrit and Ahura in one of the ancient languages of Persia. History has no real beginning or end as their concept of history was a cyclic one, just like seasons with summer and winter in perpetual interchange with each other.

> The three big western religions Judaism, Christianity and Islam have Semitic roots. The Koran and the Old Testament were written in kindred languages. It is notable that Semites believed in one deity from very early times. They also had a linear look at history. God creates the world, and from that moment onwards 'History' begins. But this shall come to an end on 'Judgement Day'. One important characteristic is also the role of 'history' itself. Man perceives that God intervenes in history, or stronger still that history only exists so that God's will is expressed.

It appears now that growing out of one another just like the motion of a pendulum, takes us in another direction. In the 21st century the world is evolved to an integrated entity. Every day more so. It is impossible today for a culture to develop without the influence of external factors. In this manner the East, the North and South will exert influences on the West and vice versa.

Whether one wants or not, one is confronted more and more with such globalisation. It is better to be prepared and have one's competences sharpened. Such mutual enrichment and broadening of mentality is a considerable strength whether for company, organisation or co-workers. As far as society is concerned the integration of cultures is a source of welfare and tolerance not to be disregarded.

One must seek similarity instead of difference as a solid starting point. After all love, hate, trust, mistrust, strength, fear, happiness, unhappiness, mother/child relation, the quest for meaning are common to all of us, but due to our individual cultural layer of varnish are expressed in diverse ways. Increase in cultural sensitivity is an endless trip around the world. There is more and more to discover. And just like any trip, what matters is not the end of the journey but the journey itself.

NOTES

1. LSC (Living Stone Cooperation) is a cooperative with primarily social objectives (Vennootschap met Sociaal Oogmerk). Since 2007, the Centre has a new partner, Cera, a Belgian-based cooperative financial Group.

2. 'Glocalisation' as a term finds its originated in the 1980's Japanese business practices and was introduced in the English-speaking world by the sociologist Roland Robertson in the 1990's. The global and the local are regarded as the two sides of the same coin as developing countries are integrating with the world economy while at the same time they are devolving power to local governments and communities.

3. 'To rule, is to foresee', Emile de Girardin, (1806-1881), French writer and politician.

4. The Sahel – from Arabic *sahil*, meaning shore, border or coast – is the boundary zone in Africa between the Sahara to the north and the more fertile region to the south, known as the Sudan (NOT to be confused with the country of the same name).

5. Made of pounded millet.

6. *Country of Mali Interim National Development Strategy: An MDG Based Framework of Action*, Columbia University School of International and Public Affairs, November 30, 2005. (Project Team: Angela Bailey, Rekha Chalasani, Amelia Chamberlain, Kari Frame, Yehia Houry, Henri L. K. Solomon)

7. 'The pleasure to discover the difference of the other', in *Cours d' esthétique,* Théodore Simon Jouffroy, (French philosopher 1796-1842), published by Jean Philibert Damiron. The quote has been used by the travel agency Tizi-Randonnées in its promotional campaign in Morocco.

8. The German term *Gestalt*, translated as "pattern" or "configuration", emerged in Austria and Germany and appeared first in the works of Max Wertheimer, Wolfgang Köhler, and Kurt Koffka (1886 – 1941).

9. *Inleiding Comparatieve Filosofie*, Ulrich Libbrecht 1995.

10. "You have the watch, we have the time".

11. Meaning *tomorrow* or *morning*.

12. The griot tradition in Mali goes back for centuries. Griots were and are poets and advisers, oral historians, mediators, spokesmen, magicians. They

perpetuate the tradition and history of a village or family. Without a griot, a king's name died with him.

13. The Belgian nun Jeanne Devos is the guiding force behind the Movement for Child domestic workers. In 2005 she was nominated for the Nobel Price for Peace.

14. Women In Need, an organisation providing housing and help to homeless families.

15. *Onevenwichtige globalisering. Deficitair Amerika en Aziatische locomotieven,* Prof em Louis Baeck, K.U.Leuven, Leuvense Economische Standpunten 2005/109

16. http://www.understandfrance.org/France/Intercultural.html, http://forum.wordreference.com/archive/index.php/t-182874.html

17. American writer, poet and philosopher (1803-1882)

18. Anthropology, psychology and economics (HR, teaching organisation, management of diversity), sociology and other social sciences.

19. The representation is inspired by spiritual models likes the buddhist Mandala and the Enneagram of the Middle East. The complex drawings are aimed at meditation, internalisation from 'outside to inside'.

20. i.a. authors Geert Hofstede, Fons Trompenaars, Shalom Schwartz, ... mapped cultural dimensions and systems as mentioned hereafter.

21. Mythology dealing with the creation and the destruction of the world of the Norse gods.

BIBLIOGRAPHY

BAECK, LOUIS: *Onze Vierkante Wereldbol,* 2003 Davidsfonds Uitgeverij ISBN 90-5826-236-7.

CALDERISI, ROBERT: *The trouble with Africa: Why Foreign Aid Isn't Working.,* 2006 Palgrave Macmillan New York.

DE MARTELAERE, PATRICIA: *Taoïsme: De weg om niet te volgen.,* 2006 ISBN 90 263 18065/97890 263 1806 1.

DEVELTERE, PATRICK: *De Belgische Ontwikkelingssamenwerking/* De vierde Pijler, 2005 Davidsfonds Uitgeverij, ISBN 90-5826-352-5.

KYNGE, JAMES: *China Shakes the World: The Rise of a Hungry Nation* 2006 (Dutch Translation: Uitgeverij Lannoo Nv, Tielt, Belgium)

LIBBRECHT, ULRICH: *Inleiding Comparatieve Filosofie.,* 1995 Van Gorcum & Comp.

MAALOUF, AMIN: *Les identités meurtriéres,* 1992 Bernard Grasset Paris.

SPENCER-OATEY, HELEN: *Culturally Speaking: Managing Rapports Through Talk Across Cultures.,* London 2000 Continuum.

STIGLITZ, JOSEPH E.: *Making Globalisation Work.,* 2006 W.W.Norton & Company, New York.

TROMPENAARS, FONS AND WOOLLIAMS, PETER: *Business across Cultures.,* 2003 Capstone Publishing Ltd England.

Same World,
Different Paths

Walks through fields of theory

IGNACE POLLET

IGNACE POLLET

SAME WORLD, DIFFERENT PATHS
Walks through fields of theory

CONTEMPLATING INTERCULTURALISM

What is culture?

Multiculturalism and cultural relativism

Terra incognita

Generation and decay

A dialectic reading of cultures

INTERCULTURALISM INVESTIGATED

National cultures

Software of the Mind

Practical lessons form Hofstede's theory

Culture and modernity

Research into values and opinions

Back to the future

Sociology's blind spot

APPLIED INTERCULTURALISM

Ex-pats, planet & profit

Our friends in the South

Interculturalism for everyone

The coconut allegory

When people from Western Europe move to other areas, they inevitably come into contact with other cultures. A mere 1 000 kilometres to the south, we notice that times for working and relaxation are different, food is prepared differently and very different efforts are required to obtain something from the local government.

The intensity of this experience will depend on the place we find ourselves, and also on the reason we have for being there. As a *tourist*, such experiences are usually noncommittal, giving us at best a good story to tell back home: waiting times, the perils of foreign food, unexpected invitations or the foibles of a fussy little bureaucrat.

As an *expat* or development worker, sent abroad temporarily by a company or development agency, we will experience the consequences of an acculturation process at a more fundamental level. People are usually sent abroad to use their physical presence to get things done that cannot be sorted out from a distance: a building permit, a concession, more efficient production, putting a development plan into action on the ground and so on. We need to know how to deal with local partners, the local authorities, local conditions. As a rule, we can count on support from a previously agreed 'deal', which we feel (partly due to the financial input) legitimates what we are doing.

However, if we decide of our own accord to go and '*do something*' in a developing country, we will find ourselves obliged to take a large number of steps all at once: proving our identity ('adventurers' cannot often reckon on much support), finding local partners, finding funding or making them available locally, conforming to the law and the government and, on top of all this, keeping ourselves going socially, mentally and physically. And all this is aimed at putting a plan into practice in a foreign environment, a plan we have come up with ourselves: manufacturing mountain bikes on the equator, cultivating organic coffee, training long-distance runners or educating disadvantaged girls ... is it all worth it? What if we are just getting in the way? Might we be raising expectations that we cannot fulfil?

Experienced entrepreneurs would say that anyone who wants to start an enterprise needs a well-defined idea, a strategy (which clearly defines the required financial, human and material resources as well as its activities, peripheral requirements, market and target group) as well as being prepared to adapt at any time if circumstances require it. Anyone who wants to do this in a foreign environment will also find himself confronted by the *intercultural aspect*. Because you need to work with local people, it is recommended to adopt an attitude that is culturally acceptable, that shows respect and evokes friendliness. This does not just mean that you need to avoid coming across as superior or dismissive, but also that you show an interest in getting to know local culture and adopt certain attitudes and forms of behaviour that make it clear that you subscribe to the ethos and value system of the culture you find yourself in.

This last point is part of the acculturation process, and is a personal experience for anyone who has to work in a foreign environment for any length of time. Good preparation certainly makes it easier, in which practical understanding of how to deal with likely situations is based on knowledge and experience gleaned from others who have found themselves in similar situations. It also requires more fundamental reflection on culture and cultures: what they are, how deeply they are rooted, how flexible they are, how easy it is to adopt them, and how different cultures can meet in a context of acting together towards a common goal.

This text is dedicated to this final aspect. We will begin by reflecting on the phenomenon of culture itself, encounters between cultures, and the renewed interest in this issue. Secondly, we will clarify what 'validated insights' can offer us when dealing with other cultures in a given context (business, tourism, development etc.). Thirdly, we will look at what practical experience can teach us about interculturalism. The business community, development aid and tourism have developed methodologies over the years to deal with other cultures constructively. In this context, we will also explore the 'coconut model' used by the LSC as a metaphor for cultural dialogue and the learning process which thus occurs. We are conscious of the fact that, given the scope of the subjects discussed, we are sometimes striding over painstakingly mapped areas of knowledge in seven league boots. Then again, this text is intended rather as a starting point for further discussion than as all-encompassing truth. Because ...

> "*Maybe nothing is entirely true, and not even this.*"
> MULTATULI, *Ideeën,* volume 1, idea 1, p. 9

1. CONTEMPLATING INTERCULTURALISM

'Incidentally, culture is too important to leave it up to teachers.'
M. VAN DER GOES VAN NATERS [1]

It would be an exaggeration to say that social scientists left culture out in the cold for decades. Nonetheless, culture was hardly a central concept. The big stories dealt with class interactions, institutions, reproductive systems, social capital and social exclusion. Culture as a field of study was mainly left to anthropologists. In sociological terms, culture tended to be something that had to be explained on the basis of economics and power relationships, rather than being able to function on its own as an independent explaining factor. However, this situation has changed. It became clear in the 1990s that social phenomena such as success on the labour market, violence, political or apolitical attitudes, gender equality, sexual mores and so on could not be explained by socio-economic relationships alone. More frequent investment in developing countries, third world tourism, the considerable increase in migration to Europe and globalisation as a whole have put the significance of culture back at the top of the agenda.

What is culture?

'Culture is... one of the most complicated words in the English language.'
RAYMOND WILLIAMS [2]

What is culture? Trying to find a definition of culture leaves us up against the characteristic limitation of any definition: either too vague, or too one-sided. Anthropologists tend to define culture as 'a system of norms and values experienced by a group (or people) as their own', or sometimes as 'a system of providing meaning'. And yet a traveller's first impression of local culture is usually linked to phenomena that can be perceived directly, such as language, food and clothing. This indicates that the term culture represents more than one layer of reality, affecting many aspects of social life.

The original (Latin) meaning of culture referred to agriculture: types of crop. It was not until the 19th century that the word culture became associated with civilisation. In the English meaning of the word at that time, it bore connotations of the affected lifestyle of well-educated elites. Gradually anthropologists and social thinkers adopted the term and it gained an increasingly broad meaning. In 1952 Kroeber & Kluckhorn noted no less than 150 definitions of the term, and added an overarching – and since then authoritative – definition of their own: "Culture consists of explicit and implicit patterns of and for behaviour, which are acquired and transferred by means of symbols that form the specific work of human groups, including their incorporation into artefacts; the fundamental nucleus of culture consists of traditional (i.e. historically derived and selected)

55

ideas and, particularly, the values attached to them; cultural systems can be viewed on the one hand as products of actions and on the other as conditioning elements with respect to further actions."[3] Unesco uses the following definition of culture: "the whole complex of distinctive spiritual, material, intellectual and emotional features that characterize a society or social group. It includes not only arts and letters, but also modes of life, the fundamental rights of the human being, value systems, traditions and beliefs" This definition has more or less been canonised in the form of the Mexico Declaration (August 1982)[4].

In these definitions, certain elements that are typical of culture catch the eye. Firstly, we see that everything classified as culture is *of human origin*. In that sense, culture is the opposite of nature. Secondly, culture refers to those human activities that are not concerned with keeping oneself and the human species alive, but with relationships between people; in other words, it does not meet a biological or economic need but a *social need*, and the need to express this[5]. Thirdly, it is not only a matter of societies or civilisations, but also all kinds of *groups*: besides European or Chinese culture, we might speak of youth culture or organisational culture (e.g. a certain company might represent a very competitive culture, which relates to both its 'values' and the behaviour it expects from its employees)[6]. Fourthly, culture entails an element of *stability*: cultures are tough, and don't change readily. Cultures keep themselves going for a long time, generations even, because people are conditioned in them from childhood.

In other words, it is easier to explain how culture works than what it is: it is something people learn, it is social as it concerns people's relationships with each other, it is complex and stable. Moreover, it is an *invisible* and largely subconscious phenomenon, which leads to the tendency to talk about it in metaphors. Culture is to people what water is to fish. Fish only notice how essential water is to them when they find themselves stranded on dry land. For most people, culture is an environment that seems to be a matter of course, almost like nature itself. However, this changes when people move to a different location, whether or not they choose to do so, or when they make an upwards or downwards jump in social mobility, or sometimes even when different generations clash. Contact with another culture can lead to reflection on one's own culture, which then seems less a matter of course. The layered nature of a culture is sometimes clarified by portraying it as an onion or – as illustrated elsewhere in this text – as a coconut.

Multiculturalism and cultural relativism

Contemporary concepts directly linked to culture are interculturalism and multiculturalism. Just as with the term culture itself, there is often a tendency in everyday language to use these terms in a way that is appreciative or normative rather than to indicate neutral phenomena. Just as a 'cultured person' is often understood to be someone interested in intellectual activities and art, intercultural and multicultural often have the connotation of 'good', 'promoting understanding between different peoples' etc. Just like democracy and sustainability, these words have become all-encompassing terms. However, this is wishful thinking. An automatically normative interpretation of inter- and multiculturalism disguises the historical fact that cultures coming into contact with each other can just as easily be a source of confrontation and conflict as enrichment for the various parties involved. This is why we recommend a neutral and simple definition of these terms. Interculturalism: the collective activity (projects, training, artistic productions etc.) of people originating from different cultures. Multiculturalism: the shared life of people originating from different cultures within a defined geographic area.

A *'multicultural society'* alludes to the co-existence of *several cultures*. Whether they continue to co-habit the same space, or grow towards each other and end up merging into a single culture remains a subject of debate, where the distinction between people's wishes and hard facts is often forgotten. Referring to the United States or Brazil as examples of 'melting pots' just as often provokes the reaction that distinct cultures continue to exist there side by side in the form of one dominant culture and different subcultures. Nonetheless, exploring the existence of different cultures that do not all profess to enlightenment ideals and at the same time have to undergo a critical process due to mutual confrontation is a step forward in thinking about culture. It is more nuanced than the (technical, Western) tradition of *linear reasoning*, where the tacit assumption is made that other cultures will follow the same route sooner or later. It is also more concrete than the long-cherished idea of *cultural relativism*, in which each culture is seen as a reasonably balanced and complete system. This respectful attitude[7] inevitably came up against the universal pretensions of human rights. A famous example that came into sharp focus is that of the tradition of burning widows on funeral pyres in ancient India, a custom that was banned by the British in the name of human rights. A contemporary question is that of the traditional female circumcision that is still widely practiced in many countries of the Sahel. One should realise that this confrontation between different standpoints is a decidedly Western debate, a drama written by Westerners as it were, where the voice of the 'East' or the 'South' can only be heard in the places and in the ways that the script allows. The idea of a universal culture as expressed in the Universal Declaration of Human Rights is a product of Enlightenment thought. However, this is also the location of cultural relativism, based on the ideal of tolerance for other values and attitudes. This paradox can only be explained by the fact that, here too, ideas of 'respect for what exists' and 'ideas about how it should be one day', are pushed together into a single philosophy. It also teaches us that thinking about other cultures and culture in general is difficult, because we cannot avoid thinking from the perspective of our own culture.

The traditional opposite to cultural relativism is of course ethnocentrism, the tendency to view events and attitudes from the perspective of one's own value system. This debate seems to have reached a stalemate, though this is changing as the world gets smaller. Multicultural society and globalisation are forcing people to interact with each other:

you have to come to an understanding with your neighbours if you want things to run smoothly. Neither high-minded morality, exaggerated respect nor *guidelines* seem to offer a practical solution here. Conversely, people – and not only the anti-globalist movement for that matter – are afraid that the kaleidoscope of cultures may become flattened and valuable customs and expressions may disappear. Another risk is that, driven by the conviction that one's own perspective is the right one, increasing arrogance in the 'conversation' between cultures will end up making conversation impossible. In this way collective insecurity can turn into collective frustration and enmity, where beliefs about oneself and others get stuck in self-fulfilling clichés.

Terra incognita

If we avoid falling into the trap ourselves of arrogantly seeking out new guidelines which by nature would be ethnocentrically-driven, it would seem sensible to gain an overview of the body of knowledge relating to 'culture and cultures', incomplete as it is. We will soon see that there is in general precious little consolidated knowledge of culture and cultures – what they are, where they come from, how they work internally and with respect to other cultures.

When talking about *culture in itself*, it is convenient to distinguish between the static and dynamic elements of cultures. The *static* (or synchronic) approach observes culture in itself, whether a certain culture (in a given time and place) or the general phenomenon of culture. A certain amount of knowledge does exist here. Philosophers, anthropologists, sociologists and a range of other experts in the field have been asking for 150 years what culture is and what makes it culture. The attitudes that led, after Sir Francis Galton, to cultures being linked to racial characteristics, which were moreover classified as superior or inferior, are far behind us[8]. It is now generally accepted that a culture is a layered phenomenon, with the nucleus or bottom layer being linked to values and beliefs, and the outermost or uppermost layers linked to behaviour, modes of interaction and their expression in language, art and transferred 'heritage'. Culture manifests itself most clearly in customs that we see in daily life (eating, housing, clothes, work, sex etc.) and in customs we see expressed for fundamental rites of passage (birth, initiation, marriage, death etc). Anthropologists and ethnographers have come a long way since the time of Margaret Mead, Lévi-Strauss and Malinowski. There are few regions, peoples, metropolises or tribes left whose culture has not been mapped. Anthropologists have also made frequent and useful attempts to look beyond the ends of their noses. Relationships confirmed between the members of a community have led to attempts to establish codes that might apply at a higher level or within related communities. Some of them have gone even further and tried to explain 'modern' behaviour from the perspective of base patterns of 'primitive' behaviour. The underlying explanation, in analogy to the behaviour observed in animals, is often sought in evolution theory, the survival of the fittest – whether the fittest individual or species. Desmond Morris is someone who has popularised these insights, but his absolutist presentation of this 'social Darwinism' is strongly contested.

Anthropological research methodology has long since been directed at the intensive study of small-scale social connections. The question is, however, whether that approach is also suitable for researching large-scale, complex societies. This is why anthropological insights are taken up by sociologists and psychologists in wider contexts, which has led to areas of study such as comparative sociology and cross-cultural psychology. And yet it is Hofstede's approach in particular that has offered new insights into the nature of culture and cultural differences. Hofstede used a quantitative method (large-scale surveys, in this case questionnaires administered to employees of IBM in more than 50 different countries), which particularly shed light on dimensions of culture that could be combined to characterize national cultures. We will discuss Hofstede and a number of related researchers such as Hall, Trompenaars, Hampden-Turner and Schwartz more extensively in the following chapter.

The *dynamic elements* of culture have been studied far less, not least because the subject does not easily lend itself to research. Studying the 'dynamic elements' of cultures means asking questions like: what is the origin of cultures, how did they come into being? How transferable are cultures to population groups (e.g. in the regions conquered by the Romans or by the Arabs after the rise of Islam)? How do cultures change or reproduce? At a first glance, a considerable amount of historical research appears to exist, but most historians are more concerned with the history of states and events as the object of their research. This means that there has been sufficient attention to the rise and fall of states and empires. Nonetheless, the groundbreaking work by the French *Annales school* (Braudel, Le Roy Ladurie, Duby etc.) turned historians' gaze away from the 'great figures in history' (Julius Caesar, Genghis Khan, Napoleon and so on) and focussed it on the development of anonymous groups with respect to their environment. Attention was paid to structures that offered explanations (navigation routes and trade flows) as well as to 'little histories' and diachronic historiography (e.g. concerning nutrition habits, the division of labour, mining, musical instruments etc.). For Braudel, geography is an important explanatory factor for the customs of population groups in a given period. Other historians in this school (Lucien Fèbvre, Michelle Vovelle etc.) come closer to defining 'culture' as a historical (i.e. changeable and dynamic) category when they take 'mentality' as their subject of study. The history of mentality, according to these authors, is the history of attitudes, behaviour and unconscious collective assumptions on the part of societies and social groups defined in time and space. As relevant and enriching as this is, however, it cannot give us any fundamental explanatory insight into the dynamics of culture.

Generation and decay

Some cultural anthropologists have gone a step further than making ethnographic 'maps' of social and tribal groups, and in doing so have bridged the gap with philosophical anthropology, seeking factors that form universal keys to civilisation. Claude Lévi-Strauss took inspiration from the methods of linguists (Jakobson) to apply the concept of structure to basic human phenomena such as relationships. In his first major work on kinship structures[9], he proposes the taboo on incest as a starting point for communication and exchanges of women between groups, which he sees as a criterion for the transition from nature to culture.

It is only a small step from philosophical anthropology to philosophy itself, where the strength of conviction is no longer rooted in refutable 'evidence', but rather in the conclusive nature of the argumentation itself. Searching in philosophy for a learning system that allows changes to be explained as such (and not as a result of a certain postulated fundamental motor, such as the economy, the drive to power, great ideas, God etc.), inevitably leads to dialectics. Dialectics are often associated with Marx' vision of dialectical materialism (which was intended to buttress his thinking on economics), but in fact dialectics do not belong to any single philosopher. From what existed more or less in ancient Greece as a form of argumentation (proving something with reference to its opposite), dialectics evolved into a method of perceiving, indicating[10] and predicting changes in human reality. The philosopher Hegel went as far as to elevate the method to the status of reality itself, as it unfolds. Hegel worked on the assumption that everything in existence was related. With a strong belief in this single 'spirit' that encompassed the entire universe, Hegel was not only a holist but also an 'idealist' in the literal sense, as opposed to a materialist: it is not matter, but ideas that make up reality. In contemporary terms, we would say that

Hegel was not concerned so much with events themselves but with perception of them. Marx reversed this reasoning and took physical nature as a starting point, with humanity as part of nature. He claimed that nature is used against humanity through appropriation and exploitation by a single class, and needs to be regained by humanity. This would supposedly only happen in a classless society, with a revaluation of human labour as the highest emanation of nature. Through this way of reasoning, Marx placed himself in a for that time new school of thought: dialectical materialism. This materialism was expressed, for example, in the cultural policy of the USSR and Maoist China, where the proletariat and recognisable worldly conventions set the tone, and everything that hinted at intellectualism was suspect and 'reactionary'. Marx also used the dialectic method to explain the principles of the value of labour, the class struggle and political history. However, it is Marx' theory of the constantly returning concentration of capital from competition to monopoly that has survived the test of empiricism most clearly, which moreover remains contemporary (see Microsoft) and has kept the suspicion alive that 'capitalist economy' leads to the opposite of the elements upon which it was founded: freedom and development.

A dialectic reading of cultures

A philosopher who has approached the dynamics of culture through dialectics is René Girard. Girard's work[11] encompasses far more than this one aim, and so our attempt to reproduce it will take a shortcut, so to speak. According to Girard, a particularity of culture is the fact that it restricts violence within a society. Irrelevant of how they arose, societies require an element of order that takes the form of mass mimesis: people imitate each other in the way they work, build a house, choose a partner etc.. This mimesis ensures recognition and identity, but also always entails the risk that imitated individuals will feel that their uniqueness is threatened and end up wanting to kill the imitator. After all, there is a desire in every individual for 'selfhood' and 'distinctness', a need to be recognised and appreciated. If a shoemaker's neighbour becomes a shoemaker too, this may evoke the shoemaker's friendship (due to recognition), but also rivalry. This immanent threat of internal violence is only deflected by the mechanism of sacrifice. Violent energy is directed at a scapegoat which may be a person or people with characteristics that deviate from the norm: a different ethnic origin, a disability, or twins, for example. This scapegoat is to be sacrificed in the presence of the gods or god. Because mass mimesis is constantly expanding, and hence the threat of violence is increasing, the sacrifices need to be multiplied as well. Rituals are 'scheduled' in order to prevent unpredicted violent outbursts. Likewise, individual lives are punctuated by 'rites of passage' (to manage the crisis of adolescence) and death rites. However, if this sacrifice mechanism is used too gratuitously, it loses its meaning and an increasingly fragmented society no longer feels involved in the ritual. Girard calls this the crisis of sacrifice: the scapegoat trick no longer works. This leads to an internal weakening of the society and what used to be its survival mechanism gradually becomes the mechanism of its downfall. If we transposed Girard's reasoning to the contemporary situation, we would see a form of mimetic rivalry on world scale in globalisation: the 'standardized sausage'. The media as well as the internet would then be the 'gods' who are becoming increasingly accessible and hence less credible. Institutions that fail and need to be replaced at an ever-increasing speed (the UN, the European Union, governments etc.) form the crisis of sacrifice. As these institutions lose contact with their democratic basis, they are also losing their universal meaning.

The question here is whether we are not being caught in the trap of 'applying the small to the large'. Girard derives his argumentation from his extensive knowledge of ancient cultures (including Greek, Jewish and early Christian culture) and their myths, customs and way of dealing with religion and violence. Girard has plenty to say about the survival mechanism, but less about the reason why cultures arise[12] (why this culture and no other?) and even less about the interactions and clashes between cultures. And yet Girard's works, and more generally a dialectic reading of cultures, contain important lessons. Cultures, so we see, are reproduced in an almost compulsive manner and maintained from a principle of the group's will to survive. In other words, a culture's survival mechanism teaches us something about its origin. Religion has often played an important role in this maintenance attribute. Central to Roman Catholic culture, for example, is the cult of sacrifice: a victim can depend on protection; suffering is virtuous. We might suspect that this is based on the earliest, underground Christian movement where only those who were visibly weaker could be trusted. The suffering figure of the sacrificial victim survives because he is not dangerous. Anyone who gained a high profile must have been someone who knew how to keep on the right side of the Roman overlords. Islamic sexual mores provide another example. They are often sharply criticised in the West because of their distinct gender differences. Men are allowed to do many things (although not everything), whereas women are not. However, Islam arose on the Arabian peninsula, where a large number of small tribes were constantly at war with each other. The sexual availability of women was seen as crucial for the survival of the group. This took the form of polygamic systems, or in more extreme cases the toleration of rape when inflicted upon an unaccompanied woman. Infighting within the group was avoided by the fact that there were also strict internal rules. This phenomenon was generally present, incidentally, among small communities in undefined territories such as desert regions, even in the time before Islam.

Something else we can deduce from Girard's thinking is that clashes with the outside world are not the only reason why cultures disappear. The survival mechanism also demonstrates the weak point of the culture in question. It is often internal fragmentation and disintegration that sound the death knell.

Confrontations or dialogue between cultures can also be indicated in an existential manner. Following in the footsteps of Emmanuel Levinas[13], an intercultural relationship can also be defined as an asymmetric relationship. The other imposes him/herself on me: the issue at stake is not so much the culture but the encounter itself. I did not ask for that hand to be extended to me, and my primary reaction is one of fear resulting in fleeing behaviour or ignoring the gesture – or violence. According to Levinas, this asymmetry is removed by the presence of a third party: God, institutions, or a political forum. We do realise the otherness of the other, but we cannot comprehend it, or to take it even further, we cannot maintain the pretence of comprehending it. A way out of this impasse is that of acceptance, which is not the same as empathising with or classifying the other. Dialogue could be aimed at 'containing' possible conflicts and allowing each party their value. This may initiate a process whereby we learn to encounter each other in a state of openness, without seeing the other as a carrier of particular characteristics. Hence this dialogue teaches each party what their own identity is, and how they can act on it where necessary.

. . .

The most important finding of this philosophical discussion is still that modesty is called for with respect to knowledge of how cultures grow and decay. This applies to interculturalism as well, both at collective and individual level. Even the distinction between the collective and the individual is not obvious. People from different cultures do have their individual characteristics, but they are also 'carriers' of cultures. Frequently the other is mainly perceived in this second capacity. People may begin with certain expectations of how the other will behave and anticipate this. But it is also possible to break through this 'expected protocol', remaining oneself, directing one's attention towards other characteristics of the person one is speaking to (gender, age, profession etc.). We do have this freedom. On the basis of their experiences, people end up assuming certain attitudes that they feel comfortable with, or that they find most useful to their task. This does not necessarily mean the most comfortable form of interaction from the perspective of their conversation partner. But given the existing knowledge of culture, we cannot offer an approach as *one best way*.

2. INTERCULTURALISM INVESTIGATED

'Vérité en deçà des Pyrénées, erreur au-delà'
BLAISE PASCAL

National cultures

Intercultural encounters are as old as the existence of cultures themselves. In prehistory, ancient times and the early Middle Ages, such encounters were mainly an aspect of *migrating populations* and confrontations between nomadic and sedentary communities. Indeed, the first great empires (Persia, Macedonia, Rome) had to find ways of coping with their *subjects* who needed to be pacified and employed in the army or as slaves, to keep the empire manageable. Moreover, there have been trade links between peoples almost since the dawn of time, with most societies granting traders and trading parties a separate status.

Intercultural contacts have multiplied in modern times, particularly the last few decades, and we find them in different social sectors. First there was *colonisation* and a minimal integration of the colonised peoples into nation states. This was paired with *missionary work* and organisation of the colonised regions by the church. Another aspect was the extraction of natural resources by major companies, who needed to use local labour. After the Second World War and decolonisation, the *business and trade system* of the North well and truly descended on the South, which was soon revealed as a consumer market or cheap production market.

At the same time, a steadily rising wave of *migrants* arose. *Development aid* was another area of intercultural contact. And finally, in the wake of the hippies travelling to places like Goa and Nepal in search of enlightenment, *tourism* has extended to 'faraway destinations inhabited by foreign peoples'. All this has contributed to an increased interculturalism, not to mention a wave of fashionable exoticism.

As this occurs, we are confronted with the increasingly urgent need to communicate with each other better, more respectfully and also more effectively and efficiently. Validated knowledge and practical *guidelines* based on this knowledge are certainly useful. Despite the abundance of how-to-do-it texts in management literature, overarching academic approaches are thin on the ground. Anthropologists tend to limit themselves to case studies. Logical-positivist scholars[14] have always had difficulties with the methodological unit for culture. An initial question is what exactly you are supposed to be measuring. Can culture be measured in the form of values, customs, achievements? In practice we find that scientists usually end up with dimensions of culture, in other words parameters that group a number of values in the form of clear opposites (e.g. individualism versus collectivism). A second question is where to take the measurements. Are cultures considered to be the same as nationalities, or should measurements be taken at a higher or lower level?

Although scientists have always left the possibility of local (e.g. Bavarian) or meta-national (e.g. Latin) culture open, they often opt for nationalities as the unit of measurement, for pragmatic methodological reasons. A person's nationality is usually easy to determine. Moreover, nationalities have not generally come about by coincidence, and it is likely that people of a given nationality generally adhere to the same values and norms as their compatriots. In a certain sense, Belgium is a good example of this. It is often said the Flemish share a language with the Dutch but that their culture is different: both have a strong work ethic, but the Flemish tend towards a more pleasure-loving lifestyle and prefer to play it safe, whereas the Dutch are more calculating and also more inclined towards adventurousness, for example, they are more inclined to emigrate. With respect to French-speaking Belgians, the Flemish speak a different language but their culture is more or less the same, with both groups sharing a dislike of authority. This means that there is such a thing as a Belgian culture, mainly characterised by a strong feeling of being the underdog: it is better not to stand out too much. This surely has something to do with the many centuries of foreign rule that preceded Belgian independence, when rulers could impose taxes at will, recruit men for the army or subject the population to punitive expeditions. People who stood out put themselves at risk.

The above illustration sounds like a cliché, and indeed it only applies if you observe the average values, norms and attitudes of sufficiently large groups. The dimensions set here for cultures are not necessarily reflected in the behaviour of each individual who belongs to this culture. Analysis at cultural level, in other words, has no predicative value for individual behaviour[15].

The anthropologist Ruth Benedict[16] classified cultures as cultures of shame and cultures of guilt, on the basis of differences she had observed in emotional dispositions between Japan and Western countries. But it is Edward T. Hall[17] who has the honour of being one of the first who sought out explanatory dimensions of culture. He distinguishes 'high context' cultures from 'low context' cultures. High context means that there is little need to make things explicit when communicating, because the message is already present in the environment or the person's assumed prior knowledge. In a 'high context' situation, there may be many silences, or a lot of talking 'beside the point' will be done. Low context means that the information is contained in an explicit code. This dimension explains differences between national cultures. The USA and Germany tend to be 'low context': knowledge is explicit, generated consciously and accessible to everyone. Relationships between people are loose, open, often short-term and functional. Asian, African and Latin cultures tend to be 'high context': knowledge is implicit and difficult for outsiders to understand. Relationships are personal and more long-term.

In her autobiographic novel *Fear and Trembling,* Amélie Nothomb relates how, as a young Western woman, she took on an internship at a Japanese company. One of her tasks was to bring the coffee during management board meetings. One day she made the 'mistake' of replying to a remark made to her. She was demoted to cleaning lady on the spot. According to the (high) context, she was not supposed to understand Japanese, let alone reply to the remarks of her superiors. Nobody had told her this: she was supposed to deduce it from the context.

High and low context do not only apply to national cultures. An evening playing cards with a fixed group of friends in a low context culture (such as most Northern European cultures) is usually high context: everyone knows what and how to play, when to take a break, what happens to the kitty etc. An airport is almost always low context: check-in queues, boarding and luggage arrangements are indicated explicitly in Asia and Africa as well. However, the fact that one is in a high context culture becomes clear if something goes wrong, for example if a flight is delayed or cancelled. Westerners are often dismayed or enraged to find that all the rules suddenly disappear. The friendliness one shows in dealing with the staff behind the counter may be a determining factor in the chance of getting an alternative flight as quickly as possible.

Taking high and low context into account has demonstrated its value for all kinds of intercultural communication. Whether the situation is negotiation or a scientific lecture at a congress, in a low context culture the rule applies: be on time, keep to the timing and the prior arrangements and – above all – get to the point quickly. In a high context culture, it is more important to let several people have their say, even if they have nothing new to make known. People don't really mind if a speaker greatly exceeds his or her allotted time. But it would be inappropriate to interrupt the speaker or criticise them in a way that results in a public 'loss of face'.

As to positioning in terms of nationality, the dichotomy of high or low context generally corresponds to the dichotomy of collectivist or individualist cultures.

Hall also used the dimension of monochronic and polychronic cultures. This refers to the use of time in relation to interpersonal contacts. Monochronic means that time arrangements must be respected at all costs, tasks must be completed one by one and personal relationships subordinated to the tasks. Polychronic means the opposite: people do lots of tasks at once; personal reasons allow arrangements to be cancelled without informing the other person and the agreed time scheme has no more than an indicative value. Hall's dimensions are not based on empirical research, but they do correspond to the experiences of the many people who have tried to communicate or negotiate across cultures. His work was a step towards a more systematic and empirically based theory. Such a theory would soon be developed.

Software of the mind

The great breakthrough for dimensions of national culture was to come in the shape of the IBM research project by Geert Hofstede (*Culture's Consequences*, 1980; *Software of the Mind*, 1991)[18]. This project has since become famous. Hofstede derived his cultural dimensions from a survey of work-related values and attitudes among a good 100 000 IBM employees in more than 50 countries. The first survey was carried out around 1970 (it took several years to collect all the data). When the study was reproduced at a later date, the number of countries was increased to a total of 85. Hofstede used a questionnaire with fairly de facto

questions concerning all kinds of values, attitudes and beliefs that the respondents might have about their work,
with closed response categories (to enable statistic analysis).
Factor analysis was applied to the data processing, a pro-
cedure where the questions whose answer patterns correlate are combined into a single factor. Hofstede originally
discovered four factors that became four cultural dimensions. These dimensions cannot be reverted to each other
and are therefore not predefined. Moreover, multivariate
analysis has shown that they are not the result of underlying morphological characteristics (gender, age, social class
etc.) either. Hofstede indicates the cultural differences he
finds as a mental programming that has been formed over
the centuries: the *software of the mind*.

The first dimension is *power distance*, which is the extent to which it is expected and accepted for power to be
distributed unevenly. This is expressed in the answers to
questions: do you dare to disagree with your superior? Do
you trust your superior's judgement when important decisions are being made, or should the decision be considered by the group? A lower power distance index and thus
a more 'pro-equality' attitude can be found in the North
European countries (including Germany[19]) and the Anglo-
Saxon countries. A higher power distance index (and hence
a 'pro-hierarchy' attitude) can be observed in Eastern Europe, China, Latin America and to a lesser extent in Africa,
the Arab world and the Latinate European countries. An
important parameter that crosses the dimension of power
distance is people's level of education: even in countries
with a low power distance, poorly educated people are

more likely to be 'pro-hierarchy'. Hofstede speculates that the origins of cultural differences in these terms may lie in a combination of climate and the history of the state. People in colder climates have learned to rely on themselves and not to put too much trust in their rulers In warmer climates with a bountiful soil, hierarchical balance was the best way of preventing 'someone else' from laying claim to one's 'own' piece of land. Another possible cause is whether or not a country has belonged to a large centralist empire (the Roman Empire, China etc.). Central authority assumes the presence of a population who is prepared to take orders from the centre: *quod licet Iovi, non licet bovi*[20].

The second dimension that emerges from Hofstede's factor analysis is, recognisably, *individualism / collectivism*. A society is individualist if the bonds between individuals are loose and people are only expected to look after themselves and their close family. Collectivism, on the other hand, means that people are included from birth in close groups that offer lifelong protection in return for unconditional loyalty. In general, all Western countries are individualist, Asia and Africa more collectivist and Latin America is extremely collectivist. Japan's score is in the middle (as it also does for power distance). Work-related values that indicate individualism include attaching importance to free time, having freedom and autonomy at work, challenging work etc. Individualist cultures are usually low-context: interpersonal activities require an explicit code. This is why contracts have such a high value in the West: *pacta sunt servanda*[21]. Privacy is another aspect: the right to personal space. Cultures with high power distance indexes are often collectivist, but not always: France, for example, is highly individualist. In collectivist cultures, a large part of the interpersonal ethos is built around the prevention of loss of face. Loss of face means that one cannot meet the demands made as a result of one's social position. Hofstede assumes that in the beginning, only collective cultures existed. Individualism became lodged *in the minds* as a result of increasing wealth and urbanization.

Masculinity / femininity is the third dimension, which should not be confused with notions of gender at the individual level. A culture is masculine if the social gender roles are clearly distinct: men tend to be more assertive, hard and focused on material success, and women tend to be more modest, tender and focused on care and quality of life. A culture is feminine if social gender roles overlap: both men and women are considered to have ambitions to personal success as well as being caring and focused on quality of life. Hofstede mainly found indications of this in the answers to questions in the survey concerning work motivation: why people go to work, what is important to them at work: income and career, or rather the atmosphere, colleagues and possibility of combining it with family life. It appears that Japan is a highly masculine culture, and China, the Anglo-Saxon countries and the German-speaking countries are also fairly masculine. The Latin and Slavic countries, and most of Asia and Africa tend to be somewhere in the middle, or divided. The Netherlands and Scandinavia are highly feminine. This dimension is to some extent affected by age: young people in all cultures tend to have more masculine values (in favour of distinct gender roles: *boys will be boys*) whereas older people (both men and women) tend to have more feminine values. Hofstede sees a link with religion here: masculine cultures concur with 'ruling' as a central tenet (Sunni Islam, Catholicism, Japanese Buddhism) and feminine cultures with 'suffering' as a central tenet (Shiite Islam, Protestantism, Hinayana Buddhism). However, he also believes that feminine cultures have historically arisen in cultures exposed to long periods of peace and prosperity.

The fourth dimension, and by no means the least important in the light of interculturalism, is the *avoidance of uncertainty*. Hofstede defines the avoidance of uncertainty as the extent to which members of a culture feel threatened by unfamiliar situations. This feeling may be expressed by nervous tension and the need for predictability: protocol, informal and formal rules. Societies which greatly avoid uncertainty are the Latin countries, the Slavic countries and – to a lesser extent – Japan and Korea. The Arab countries and German-speaking countries score average. Uncertainty is more tolerable in Africa, Anglo-Saxon culture and most of all in Scandinavia and China, Taiwan, Vietnam and Singapore. 'Avoidance of uncertainty' sounds pejorative, as if it referred to a culture of cowards, but it is mainly characterised by legal certainty (authority is invested in laws rather than people) and expressiveness (it is socially acceptable to show emotion). Cultures that tolerate uncertainty are often boring and sombre. Avoiding uncertainty does not mean avoiding risks: it does not mean that risks are limited, but that ambiguousness is reduced. In work-related terms, we mainly see the avoidance of uncertainty in more frequent stress at work, a preference for fixed company rules and a preference for staying with the current employer for a long time. Moreover, Hofstede indicates that security is more likely to be an important political issue in cultures that avoid uncertainty and there is also a greater chance of xenophobia. In cultures that tolerate uncertainty there is a greater chance that people with different convictions can still be personal friends. In historical terms, Hofstede partially locates the avoidance of uncertainty in the system of laws of the Roman Empire (which was absent in the Chinese Empire). He admits that there is no direct and conclusive explanation for many national scores for avoiding uncertainty.

Hofstede adds a fifth dimension in his later work. The dimension *short-term/long-term oriented* is the result of collaboration with the Canadian Michael Bond, who carried out a Chinese Value Survey for 23 countries in the Pacific region. Hofstede's first three dimensions could be clearly identified in this study, but avoidance of uncertainty was not obvious. Another dimension appeared in its place, which was clearly related to the practical ethics of Confucius[22]: the extent to which people aim for future reward, particularly by means of tenacity and frugality. The CVS study and replicated studies indicated that the following countries score highly for this dimension: China, almost all East Asian countries, India and Brazil[23]. Scandinavia, Benelux and France scored average, followed by Germany, Poland and Italy. Countries that are clearly oriented to the short term are the Anglo-Saxon countries, Zimbabwe, Nigeria and Pakistan. External signs of short-term orientation are 'keeping up with the Joneses', showing off one's wealth and status that is based mainly on money. Another sign is the percentage of the population in prison (e.g. in the USA). Being short-term oriented means trying to solve today's problems using traditions associated with the origins of the nation: religious fundamentalism (increasingly in Islamic countries), traditionalism (in Africa) and free initiative and 'market fundamentalism' (e.g. in the USA, Canada and Australia). Long-term orientation is often expressed in the broad mandate given to the government to address questions of collective importance.

Practical lessons from Hofstede's theory

The classification of these national cultures according to cultural dimensions composed from statistical analyses put Hofstede in a risky position in an extremely sensitive area: national pride on the one hand and the fact in itself of finding culture so significant ('mental programming') on the other. Indeed, there was no lack of *criticism*. The survey was only taken among employees of IBM. Nonetheless, this limitation can also be seen as an advantage: it neutralizes possible variations due to differing social backgrounds (which would be the case if the sample would contain e.g. mainly managers in the USA and mainly farmers in India). Another point is that it only concerned attitudes related to work. However, Hofstede argued that national cultures make themselves felt in all areas of life: family, education, work, politics etc. A third point of criticism was the timing of the survey: it was carried out thirty years ago, so haven't certain things changed? Hofstede is resolute on this point, too: cultures are deeply rooted, and have developed over centuries. They don't change in a couple of decades. And yet this may be the weak point of Hofstede's theory. His historical indications do not always come across equally convincingly, even if this in itself does not detract from the findings of his survey.

A theory is often judged by its practical value. A first point here is that in order to gain a certain degree of realism, the dimensions sketched must be put into practice. This is only possible by combining the dimensions, leading to matrix representations that allow us to use typologies.

In educational processes, for example, the main factors at play are power distance and masculinity/femininity. This leads to the following tentative types[24]:

	low power distance (equality)	high power distance (hierarchy)
feminine culture (M/F)	non-authoritarian education	(combination seldom occurs)
masculine culture (fixed role models)	"British" education	Mediterranean education

This provides an explanation of the fact that, for example, pupils at English boarding schools were often given responsibilities at a young age, but on the other hand corporal punishments were seen as appropriate for a long time. It also shows that the risk that exists for a non-authoritarian education in a masculine culture with a high power distance, the educator may experience problems of authority.

In politics, namely in terms of the different types of state, it is to be expected that both the power distance and the degree of collectivism are important. This gives the following picture:

	low power distance (equality)	high power distance (hierarchy)
collectivism	cooperative form of democracy (rare)	authoritarian states
individualism	democratic states	"statism"

The odd one out here is statism, which we mainly find in the French-speaking countries (France, Belgium, Quebec, French-speaking Switzerland). In this variant, we find individualism brought into the state, as it were. A career in government is highly desirable and businesses need to cooperate with the government for almost everything. An explanation of this 'variant' is in the fact that democracy in France has its own roots, and developed separately from the 'British' model (which has been exported far more often). At the other extreme is the cooperative model, with little structure and a 'spontaneous' feeling of belonging. The only country that belongs in this quadrant is Costa Rica (emphasis on education and health care; no army; division of power; peaceful solutions).

We find the most 'robust' application in the typology of business organisations, based on the combination of power distance and tolerance of uncertainty. This combination leads directly to *Mintzberg's company types* (added in brackets)[25].

	low power distance (equality)	high power distance (hierarchy)
tolerance of uncertainty	company as 'market' (ad hoc structure)	company as 'family' (simple structure)
avoidance of uncertainty	company as 'machine' (professional bureaucracy)	company as 'pyramid' (bureaucracy)

We mainly find the 'market' model of business in Anglo-Saxon and Scandinavian countries. The 'family' model is typical of China, East Asia, India and Africa. The 'machine' model can be found in German-speaking countries and Israel. The 'pyramid' type of business is typical of Latin countries (including Belgium), the Slavic countries and Japan. The Arab countries and Iran are not represented here (since they tend to score somewhere near the middle for everything). Mintzberg's basic forms of organisation mainly refer to the co-ordinating principle and the organ within the organisation that has the key position. In an ad hoc structure, adaptation is important and the supporting staff (e.g. the IT department) have the key to this. In a professional bureaucracy, the primary characteristic is a standardisation of skills, and those who carry out the tasks are the most important. In a bureaucracy, it is not skills but tasks that are standardised, and the accent is on the specialised staff. In a simple structure, the top is the most important and keeps control through personal supervision. According to Mintzberg, a fifth model exists (that cannot be represented in this matrix and mainly applies in the USA), namely the division structure, where middle management has the key and it is mainly results that are standardised.

The matrix above shows that management principles and 'tools' cannot simply be exported. 'Management by objectives' and participatory management don't work in cultures with a high power distance. 'Feedback talks' are difficult to deal with in collectivist cultures, where criticism of the way a task has been carried out is experienced as criticism of the person. On the other hand, it is sometimes claimed that globalisation and the presence of many companies in a foreign environment allow certain values to take root in other cultures. Hofstede does not agree with this. In the working environment (as distinct from the family or educational environment), the socialisation process in which values are learned is already complete. The only things that can be passed on are practices. If an American company wants to introduce a certain practice (e.g. quality circles based on customer feedback) to a French subsidiary, it is best to find a way of linking this practice to values in French professional life, such as communication and responsibility from a central decision-making point plus professional pride and love of the job on the part of the specialised employees. In France, respect for one's 'métier' is more highly thought of than loyalty to the employer or the high opinion of a satisfied customer. Organisational culture is a reality, but unlike national culture, it has less to do with a long-term system of values.

In order to identify a national culture, the scores in different dimensions must be taken as a whole. The relative influence that each of these dimensions exercises on the formation of a culture is not clear, however[26]. Moreover, other dimensions may exist that were not covered by questions in the original questionnaires. Hofstede is aware that the main way for his theory to gain credibility is application in practice. As an internationally renowned advisor, he has moreover played an appreciated role in company mergers. And yet his 'dimensions' still stand as empirical research, because they were not predefined but arose out of factor analysis. What is more, Hofstede falls over himself to emphasise that a score for a given dimension does not imply a moral judgement. His native country, the Netherlands scores as somewhat individualist, feminine (quality-oriented), tolerant of uncertainty (innovative) and with a low power distance (granting responsibility). A high power distance has the advantage of greater discipline. The avoidance of uncertainty leads to thoroughness and masculinity means results-oriented.

Hofstede is on particularly thin ice when he makes claims to the origins and changeability of cultures. With respect to their origins, he generally refers to climatological factors, long periods of peace and prosperity and a past under the protection of a major empire (China or the Roman

Empire). However, this is too vague to explain differences between countries. Moreover, he characterises cultures as only capable of change over very long periods of time, only to give examples of the opposite: Brazil scores as 'long-term oriented' thanks to its Japanese immigrants who have been there since about 1910 and only make up 1% of the population. He claims that a significant change of culture has occurred in Germany since 1945 with the hierarchic model being scrapped. Africa will apparently not develop because the traditional African institutions have not survived colonisation. If culture is passed on 'with a mother's milk' in educational processes, then it will indeed take several generations for values to change. But it seems that Hofstede underestimates the speed at which cultures can change, perhaps because he has no theory of the effect that cultural encounters can have on 'collective mental programming'.

Culture and modernity

In 1993, Fons Trompenaars and Charles Hampden-Turner published *Riding the Waves of Culture*[27], a handbook of coping with different cultures that was also based on an extensive survey of managers in various organisations in 39 countries. The response scores are represented by means of a classification model with seven dimensions. Trompenaars starts with the assumption that cultures are distinguished by the solutions they offer to problems relating to (1) interpersonal relationships, (2) use of time and (3) the position of people with respect to their environment. Interpersonal relations are the most important 'source' of culture here and cover five dimensions:

- *universalism versus particularism*: whether people base their decisions on general rules or more on the relationship they have with the people involved. Universalistic jurisprudence is intended to be objective, whereas particularist jurisprudence is arbitrary (and so unjust). Universalist company policy employs the same principles and strategies everywhere; particularist company policy pays attention to the local context.

- *individualism versus communitarianism*: whether we base our relationships with others on what we want for ourselves or what is best for the group? Whether individuals opt for one pool or the other is mainly determined by nationality, but also significantly by religion (with Hinduism, Buddhism and Islam as the most communitarian and Protestantism and Judaism as the most individualistic).

- *neutral versus affective*: whether people show their emotions and take them into account when conducting business with others, or whether rationality plays a role and emotions are repressed as far as possible. Germans tend to act in a neutral way, whereas Americans tend to be emotional in their professional relationships.

- *specific versus diffuse*: the extent to which we only allow others access to specific areas of our life in specific capacities, or else allow them access to several areas in several capacities at once. Do people keep their personal life separate from their professional life or is it a given that colleagues are also friends? In certain cultures (e.g. American, Australian, Dutch) people tend to be very open, because they always keep part of their lives private. A diffuse culture can be recognised by its indirect communication (e.g. English or Japanese culture). 'Cards on the table', or saying openly what you think of a colleague's work, will soon lead to a loss of face: making a matter public when it is considered to be private. Negotiations between two parties, one from a specific and one from a diffuse culture, are a delicate matter.

- *acquired versus attributed status*: this refers both to how people achieve status (by their own efforts or a family connection) and to the value that subordinates attribute to the status of their boss ('needing to prove oneself' versus 'not open to discussion').

The other two dimensions relate to the experience of time and involvement with the environment:

- *sequential versus synchronic cultures*: Trompenaars equates this with the time horizon, which can be close or distant. 'Mañana' in South America or 'Tomorrow is another day' in Africa indicate that people mainly care about the present, whereas in synchronic cultures (like China) the present is linked both to an ancient tradition and a farsighted perspective on the future.

- *internal versus external directions*: this dimension is sometimes indicated in psychology as the 'locus of control'. Internal direction means that people have the sense of having control of their own lives, whereas external direction means that other people and nature (or God) are the determining factors. Trompenaars notes external direction as dominant in respondents from China, Russia, the Middle East and South America, and internal direction more in Europe, the USA and Japan.

To a far greater extent than Hofstede, Trompenaars profiles himself as a business advisor. In his publications[28], he describes how value dimensions can be useful in marketing, human resources policy and financial policy in different cultures. He does not go as far as to offer a genuine blueprint (or 'how-to guide'), and neither does Hofstede. Both men have their consulting bureaus, which are of course unlikely to give away their recipes for success and 'company secrets' for free.

In fact Trompenaars maintains a point of departure that is both ethically loaded and useful in practice. He wishes to do away with the attitude that there is 'one best way' for management issues. He also searches for ways of reconciling the global with the local (read: ways of formulating the goals of multinationals in a local, sometimes foreign setting), in such a way that the strengths of each national culture can contribute to the aims of the whole. Empirically and conceptually, Trompenaars' study is weak, however. His survey group was very small (initially 650 units, but later extended). His dimensions are not obtained from a factor

91

analysis of his data but were set out in advance. The first five dimensions are based on the General Theory of Action by Parsons & Shills[29], a speculative theory constructed from the standpoint of a functionalist American value system. Talcot Parsons is often called the most abstract of all the theoretical sociologists. He was moreover guilty of a certain degree of ethnocentrism[30]. Parsons considered the modernisation process to be a functional differentiation: all sections of society can serve economic prosperity. The optimal attitude for this is specific, universalist, emotionally neutral and achievement-oriented (acquired status). Trompenaars derived his last two dimensions from a small-scale study by Kluckhohn & Strodtbeck[31] of closed religious communities in Southwest America.

Moreover, Trompenaars did not calibrate his data (i.e. adjust it so that it could serve as a basis for comparison in later studies). P. Smith did later apply factor analysis to Trompenaars' data, with the result that only two dimensions remained that could be distinguished from each other: (1) the individualism/collectivism dimension (and it turned out that attributed/acquired status belonged to this dimension) and (2) the universalism/particularism dimension, to which diffuse/specific also belonged to. Furthermore, a residual factor remained that indicated internal/external control (a subject's sense of having control/no control over his/her surroundings).

A fierce debate ensued between Hofstede and Trompenaars in the scientific literature, where Hofstede's theory emerged as the empirically and conceptually more elaborate of the two. Hofstede offers more insight, because his dimensions cannot be reduced into one another and are simpler to understand. Trompenaars, whose main argument was to show that Hofstede's questionnaire had also been derived from academic research and was not therefore as value-neutral as had been claimed, can be credited with bringing attention to certain important characteristics of individualist culture in the business community: its universalism (non-particularism) and specific (not diffuse) nature. In his pre-selection of dimensions, however, Trompenaars falls into the 'trap' of modernism. Honesty requires us to add that most of the 'founding fathers' of sociology constructed their insights within a modernistic paradigm (Max Weber's tendency to rationalise; the transition from mechanical to organic solidarity in Durkheim, Tönnies, Simmel etc.). T. Parsons, on whose work Trompenaars' is based, raised modernist culture (universalism, meritocracy) to something of an ideal. This approach means that almost all non-Western cultures are bundled together, which not only does them an injustice, but also conceals a large portion of reality from view.

Research into values and opinions

Other authors have entered the field since Hofstede published his first book[32]. One of them, who made a name for himself by applying a different method, is the Israeli Shalom Schwartz[33]. Hofstede mainly used statements of behaviour in his questionnaire, to which respondents could answer yes or no, whereas Trompenaars presented his respondents with behavioural dilemmas. Schwartz – who received answers from no less than 75 000 respondents – asked participants to rate 57 values in terms of their importance as guiding principles. Schwartz considered the values that correlated to each other as *value types on the individual level*: power (wealth and status), 'achievement' (succeeding in something), hedonism, stimulation (excitement and change), personal control (ability to control one's own life), universalism (equal treatment), charity (helpfulness), tradition (devout attitude to life), conformity (obedience) and security (fixed social order). These ten value types (including the value and its opposite each time) were found by Schwartz in all the countries he studied. Conservative voters will tend to prioritise the values 'security' and 'power', whereas liberals (in the Anglo-Saxon sense of the word) tend to prefer 'universalism' and 'personal control'. Religious people tend towards 'tradition' and 'conformity', with non-religious people being more in favour of 'hedonism' and 'stimulation'. A further simplification leads to *four* main attitudes to life: *self-enhancement* (ambition and the desire to succeed), *openness to change* (personal control, a varied life, hedonism), *self-transcendence* (oriented towards others and society: a charitable attitude to life, working towards social justice and equality, etc.) and *conservatism* (tradition, conformism, safety and security). The former two are oriented more towards the self, and the latter two more towards the outside world. Schwartz uses these attitudes to life as bipolar dimensions of a circular surface whose circumference is formed by the ten values summarised above. He plots national averages[34] within this circle.

The results place Poland, Hungary, the Czech Republic and Greece in the more conservative portion of the circle. Israel scores high for self-enhancement (mainly power and achievement), with Switzerland and the Netherlands getting higher scores for hedonism. Great Britain, Norway, and once again the Netherlands and Switzerland score highly for stimulation and personal control. For self-transcendence (justice and helpfulness), Finland, Sweden and once again Switzerland are in the lead. The survey mainly produced results for European countries, and incidentally certain countries (Spain, Ireland) do not stand out in any of the value types mapped.

Schwartz used values, not behaviour, to expose dimensions of culture. The advantage of this is that possible distortions due to the specific situation are eliminated. A disadvantage is that the door is opened to social desirability. Schwartz' data analysis is a considerably more convoluted process than the one used by Hofstede, leading to a loss of clarity. However, values are doubtless closer to culture than the types of behaviour that are assumed to be derived from these values. The most crucial finding is perhaps that Schwartz, who like Hofstede has a gigantic database at his disposal, confirms the hypothesis that the variation between individuals within a national culture is always much smaller than that between national cultures themselves. This does not detract from the fact, however, that consistent variations are nonetheless found within national cultures between people of different ages, genders and social classes.

Research into national cultures should not be confused with the international comparative studies of values and attitudes that have become popular in recent years. The European Value Study has been carried out roughly every 10 years since 1980 (40 000 Europeans took part in the last edition, in 1999-2000). However the emphasis there is not on cultural dimensions and cultural differences, but rather on the attitudes of Europeans towards the church, ethical issues, the importance of work, civic duty, democracy, satisfaction with one's own life, trust in institutions etc. There is also a World Value Survey, whose questions are based on the work of Inglehart, among others. Inglehart[35] presents the hypothesis of a transition from materialist to post-materialist values (the importance of freedom, personal development, personal networks, creativity and care for one's environment)[36]. Tributes to post-materialistic values are typical of highly educated Europeans born since 1945 with an intellectual profession: the class of people who direct development co-operation. The question is whether their value system makes sense to Africans with little education whose sense of a secure livelihood stretches no more than a few weeks into the future. The cultural difference between the two groups is one explanation for the surprise – bordering on irritation – of a European development worker whose African colleague suddenly 'abandons' his agricultural collective in favour of a career at the Ministry or with an international institution.

Since the 1990s, the public has regularly been exposed to opinion polls based on these 'value surveys' in the form of 'barometers'. For example, there is an annual Eurobarometer, and also a regular Asiabarometer, Afrobarometer and Latinobarometer. The results are sometimes surprising. For example, the 2002 Afrobarometer showed that Africans tend to experience group identity with respect to a professional group (farmers, traders, miners etc.) rather than an ethnic one (27% versus 25%). The barometers are based on a large database of oral interviews (1 000 to 3 000 per country, for several countries), according to a prescribed method of sampling with a standardised questionnaire. Part of the questionnaire is fixed and belongs to a time series measuring changes over time, whereas other questions are variable such as questions on the economy, standard of living, integration, democracy, personal networks, gender, the environment etc. However, the results of these surveys do not provide insight into the various cultures of the regions included.

Back to the future

The studies discussed above can mainly be located within a tradition of social psychology and community psychology. Sociological theory has been applied to a much lesser extent when attempting to put the concept of culture into operation. In traditional sociological terms, Anthony Giddens[37] considers culture to mean the values and norms of a certain group and the goods it creates. Culture is closely linked to human societies in general, but the classification that Giddens proceeds to use mainly refers to different types of society. Historically; the evolution goes from the 'hunters and gatherers' type of society through pastoral societies to agricultural societies, which acquire the nature of civilisations when they extend themselves and assume the form of states. Furthermore, he distinguishes ethnic characteristics from cultural ones, claiming that the former are purely physical. "Many popular beliefs about race are mythical. There are no clear-cut characteristics by means of which human beings can be allocated to different races."(p.282). True to sociological tradition since Durkheim and Weber, Giddens attaches greater significance to socialisation processes, patterns of interaction, classes, groups, institutions and processes of change *within* a given culture (the Western one) than to those between different cultures. In other words, globalisation and increasing multiculturalism have not changed the dominant paradigm.

Nonetheless, a number of sociologists have developed a theory in response to the new challenges of globalisation. R. Robertson[38] draws his reasoning on this issue from Parsons' theory of social systems. In this theory, there are four sub-systems that are functionally linked for the benefit of the whole: economics, politics, culture and society. Robertson mainly notes the deep cultural gulfs that are still present during the globalisation process, especially between the Christian world and Islam, the democratic (Western) countries and autocratic (Eastern) ones, and between the industrialised world (in the North) and the non-industrialised world (in the South). However, Robertson is optimistic: he believes that interdependence resulting from the economic system will lead to the world coming closer together and the emergence of a global consciousness. This is already clear from a discourse and vocabulary that have been gaining acceptance since the 1980s: 'world peace', 'human rights' and 'the international community'.

Samuel Huntington[39] *(The Clash of Civilisations*, 1996; *Culture matters*, 2000) is less optimistic. Economic progress has led to the demise of localities and nation states as a source of identity. In the 21st century, fault lines and conflicts are increasingly situated between cultures, with three dominant players involved: Western, Islamic and Confucian culture. Islamic culture in particular (with the 'umma', the community of the faithful and the duty to extend it, as its basis), draws its legitimacy from this conflict to some extent. More generally, culture can form an obstacle to developments that were taken for granted until recently, such as economic growth and political democratisation. Although Huntington takes the phenomenon of 'culture' very seriously, therefore, he treats it from the perspective of a (Parsonsian) functionalist paradigm where it is not easy to distinguish factual reality from desirable reality (from an American point of view).

Sociologists of a Marxist bent do not consider globalisation so much in terms of its cultural impact as with respect to the relationships between owners and non-owners of capital. Harvey[40] had already demonstrated in detail how these relationships are reflected in the allocation of space in cities, where class relationships are reproduced. In today's 'global village' however, the need for spatial articulation is superseded by the time factor (the cybernetic speed of profit), meaning that individual lives become fragmented and traditional groups are dispersed. M. Castells[41] has sketched this development as the transition to a new era, with swiftly changing networks and rapid changes of position: now you win, now you lose. Just like at the stock exchanges, the future is for sale today. This volatility mortgages everything long term; production takes time and is therefore a risk factor, so selling is more attractive. And yet the method of production is still capitalist in essence and profit is still made by the exploitation of natural resources and labour. Markets are not so much geographic as being extended by increasingly rapid obsolescence. This cannot do otherwise than lead to increasing polarisation of distribution of wealth. According to this way of thinking, this trend is far more significant than interculturalism and 'cultural rapprochement'.

Sociology's blind spot

We have observed the difficulty that macro-sociological approaches to culture experience in providing a productive concept (i.e. a concept with sufficient explanatory value). Some researchers use culture as a normative concept, and others use it as a collective name for the actual building blocks (norms and values). Yet others consider culture to be a by-product of the thing that really matters (in this case, the play of economic power relationships). What makes culture so difficult for sociologists? Sociology has become what it is thanks to its combination of method, theory formation and practical application. It is difficult to squeeze culture into any of these aspects.

Culture cannot simply be observed 'empirically': it must be indexed and objectified. A problem here is that, partly due to the lack of a directing theory, both the unit of measurement and the measurement value are debatable. The *unit of measurement* means the setting: where are we going to make our observations? Where does one (sub)culture end and a new one begin? Hofstede's decision to use countries as a unit of analysis and individuals as a unit of observation was originally made for purely pragmatic reasons. Later he found that the differences between countries were statistically far more significant than differences within countries. And yet one can hardly compare China with a country like Bahrain or Luxemburg. What is more, it is clear that national borders in Africa are a product of colonial power relationships, not the borderline between culture a and culture b. Hence Hofstede limited himself here to the definitions West Africa and East Africa[42]. The *measurement value* refers to the questions asked (and the specific domain, e.g. attitudes to work). The fact that attitudes to work reflect differences in the 'software of the mind' just as well as eating and sleeping customs, moral values or concepts of god, for example, is an assumption that has not been proven in itself.

Culture is problematic for sociologists in terms of theory formation as well. Sociology is primarily an explanation of the current situation, and far less a form of archaeology. Using culture as a central concept automatically raises the question of its origin and contingency (why this culture and no other?). Sociology would have to step outside its own boundaries, as it were, something that would put the legitimacy (and the associated status) of the academic corps of sociologists at risk. As to archaeology, sociologists prefer to avoid any difficulty by siding with Weber, who saw the 16th century Protestant ethic as the 'trigger' of the modernisation process, or with Marx, who described a historical 'original accumulation' in a final chapter of *Das Kapital 1*, which proceeded differently to the subsequent accumulation process that constantly reproduces itself. Even the father of system theory in the social sciences, Niklas Luhmann[43] (), is wary of giving culture a central place in 'the systems'. That place is reserved for the notion of 'communication', something for which culture provides the semantic input[44].

In terms of the practical application of sociological insights, the issue of multiculturalism is currently a very prominent one: should immigrants and their descendents integrate into Western culture? Or is it more beneficial to society for cultures to articulate themselves separately? Sociologists have not succeeded in offering a united answer here, because this comes close to an ideological reading of the immigration issue. The call for integration is entwined with participation in wealth, availability for the labour market, fear of terrorism, suburban lawlessness or the violation of human rights (e.g. the vendetta practices 'imported' from the Balkans). On the other hand, integration also implies a certain degree of dominance. Incidentally: is integration limited to external characteristics in public life or does it include the 'software of the mind'? The fear also exists that the accentuation of cultural differences opens the door to the studying of ethnic differences. The use of ethnic origin as an explanatory variable is one of the last taboos of Western sociological practice. Culture and ethnicity are indeed different things (one nurtured, the other nature), but they do often go together for one group or another[45]. Hypersensitivity to any connotation of superiority or inferiority – as unintentional as it may be – keeps every sociologist far from making any statements linked to ethnic characteristics. And yet these connotations do exist: they lead a life of their own in the form of jokes, insinuations, prejudices and social practices that may or may not be tolerated.

Sociology is a young discipline that still has to prove its productivity, preferably on the basis of social issues where findings are simple to implement (such as labour market policy), before it can deal with something as intangible as culture. Moreover, culture shock has not yet hit hard enough to force the sociologists of the world to see cultures as the building blocks of social reality, blocks which are simultaneously elementary and complex. Where sociology hesitates to take on culture as a working concept, professional practice has not waited to make use of it with the intention of applying it in specific situations. We will go into this in more detail in the following chapter.

3. APPLIED INTERCULTURALISM

In the absence of a scientifically accepted and theoretically established framework for interculturalism, people in professional life (the business community, development work, tourism) have been seeking their own approaches. In this way a corpus of insights has arisen on the basis of experience, not so much with gaining knowledge and establishing rules in mind as with learning skills and attitudes (mental adjustments). We will cover a number of these insights and the specialisations which have grown up with them (journals, knowledge centres, learning models).

Ex-pats, planet & profit

Attention to interculturalism is sometimes seen by businesses as an extension of their more general efforts towards corporate social responability. However, there are of course many businesses that have been present in the international arena for a considerable length of time. In the second half of the twentieth century, American, European and Japanese companies began to invest, look for trading partners and set up production plants in countries with a different language and culture. The view that negotiators and ex-pat managers needed to be specifically trained to live and work in a foreign environment was increasingly accepted. Gradually, experiences and inductive knowledge were linked to a more systematic input from applied psychology. In 1975, Paul S.

Adler[46] wrote an article that launched the theory of accul-taration and culture shock. He postulated that the period of adaptation to a foreign environment follows a U-curve: from initial euphoria that quickly turns to crisis as frustra-tions and uncertainties mount; subsequently a gradual re-integration takes place, where one first rediscovers one's own cultural specificity and then also learns to accept the new culture as well (autonomy or recovery phase). Finally, one reaches the stage of adaptation, where one learns to val-ue the new culture and its cultural differences. This theory has since been subjected to considerable commentary. The initial situation can be greatly varied: a poor immigrant to Europe will not feel the initial euphoria of an American ex-pat in Singapore. Moreover, if the new environment is not receptive, it is well possible for people to find themselves caught in a permanent crisis, or left to rely on oneself and a small group of others in the same situation. What is more, evidence of the U-curve turned out to be fairly weak.

In 1986, the cognitive psychologist Milton Bennett[47] devel-oped his 'Developmental Model of Intercultural Sensitivity', a theoretical framework intended to explain people's reac-tions to cultural differences. The underlying hypothesis that was accepted is that of contact conditioning: as someone's experience of cultural differences becomes more diversified and sophisticated, their competence with intercultural re-lationships will increase. This process of gaining experience occurs in phases, where each phase represents a cognitive structure that is reflected in attitudes and behaviour. The

first three phases tend towards ethnocentricity, where one takes one's own culture as a central point of reference:
- *denial* of cultural differences:only my own culture counts; no interest in other cultures
- *resistance* to cultural differences:my culture is the only good one; other cultures are felt to be a threat
- *minimisation* of cultural differences:my culture is universal; "we are all God's children"... differences are recognised but passed off as trivial

The following three phases tend towards ethno-relativism, where one's own culture is seen as one among many, not necessarily better than others:
- *acceptance* of cultural differences:one accepts that other cultures exist and a certain interest is generated; without agreeing with everything, one respects other cultures; this respect may refer to behaviour and forms of communication, but also to world views, morality and religiousness
- *adaptation*:one uses what one has learned about the other culture to communicate more effectively with people in that culture; this does not mean giving up one's own culture
- *integration:* one has learned to absorb values, attitudes and customs from another culture to such an extent that one interiorises that culture as it were; people who have lived in another culture for a long time can 'go along with' that culture after a time; one often comes across this behaviour in non-dominant minority groups, experienced expatriates and 'global nomads': in each of these groups, a certain experience of being rootless is also pos-

sible, whereby people can no longer find any real attachment to any culture.

Because they were fairly easy to understand, both the U-curve and Bennett's model were supposed to form popular starting points for a wide panoply of practical applications. At the end of the 1980s, it was found that 20-40% of all ex-pats sent out by American companies came home early[48]. Companies active at international level consequently viewed cross-cultural training increasingly as a strategic choice. The list of publications, workshops, training packs and specialised consultants on this issue is growing daily, one might say. Cross-cultural training is intended to help ex-pats absorb culture shock and increase their skills in negotiating with and leading people from other cultures. Training may be organised in many ways: through study, seminars, role-plays and experiments. According to J. Kline Harrison[49], training must concentrate first on the person's self-organisation (self-assessment, dealing with changes and stress), and then on dealing with other cultures (e.g. with the help of Hofstede's theory) and with culture-linked incidents in the workplace. It is only then that specific knowledge and skills are required (area study, language, specific culture, suitable behaviour etc.).

Today we can observe that interculturalism in the business sector is gradually becoming institutionalised. There is already a professional organisation aimed at interculturalism, called SIETAR (Society for Intercultural Education, Training and Research). SIETAR[50] is originally American, but it has branches worldwide. It intends to provide both a real and virtual forum for dialogue and exchanges, operating through websites, event hosting and academic conferences. ITAP[51] is a consultancy group with a mission greatly inspired by Hofstede's ideas, which offers training and mentoring on interculturalism in an HRM context. In many countries, cross-cultural training is offered by management schools and language institutes (e.g. Berlitz). These are just a few examples of specialised groups aimed specifically at businesses. But how does it work in the non-profit sector?

Our friends in the South

Development aid is a system. The origin of the many players in development work (mainly international organisations, governmental agencies and NGOs) is widely varied. They originate in early missionary work, colonial policy implementation, post-war reconstruction groups, left-wing ideological groups, the new social movements (including the green movement) and are sometimes even an offshoot of commercial initiatives. Despite their diversity, an outsider senses a certain homogeneity in the system: the jargon, the profile of the people who work in the sector, the material context and opinions are very similar. As a sector, development aid has built up a fairly good reputation with the general population. Most NGOs are constructed around two poles: a campaigning function directed towards its own followers and sometimes the wider public, and work in the South that is mainly concentrated on a number of partners. Formerly, it was mainly technically skilled people (often agronomists, doctors, nurses and educators) who were sent out to provide direct support to the target group. Nowadays, there are organisations on the spot (also called NGOs) which provide the technical support, with the Northern 'co-operator' (development jargon for 'ex-pat') following up the partners at regional level, which boils down to making project proposals and reports together and solving all kinds of problems. The governmental agencies (such as DFID in the U.K and GTZ in Germany) and a number of major international institutions (such as the World Bank and the European Union's development agency) prefer to work with governments in the South, which is known as bilateral aid. Together they form the 'donor community', but this does not mean that there is much consultation between donors. Each donor, whether a governmental agency or an NGO, has sovereign decision-making power over both the choice of programme and partners, with whom they often have very personal bonds based on loyalty. The most striking internal development *within* the development aid system is the increasing weight (since the 1980s) of relief organisations, which are deployed with increasing regularity for both natural and human disasters in the South (famine in Ethiopia, emergency aid and reconstruction after the tsunami in Asia, wars in Afghanistan, the Lebanon etc.).

This system is currently under pressure. Other sections of society are raising an increasing number of questions as to the added value of NGOs and bilateral aid. 'Structural aid' in particular is under fire[52]. Organisations are encouraged to concentrate on increasing their internal professionalism and enlarging their scale. This pressure is brought to bear on both NGOs and governments in the South, where the latter often play a role as 'agents' in the implementation of World Bank funded PRS (Poverty Reduction Strategy) or other donor programmes. A whole economy of knowledge has grown up around the development sector, mainly offering training, feasibility studies, facilitation, monitoring and evaluations[53]. This knowledge sector in turn is subjected to criticism for creaming off too much of the funding donated by the generous people of the North to those in the South. What is more, NGOs – who often point an accusing finger at the world of politics, the business community and the financial system – are taken to task for their lack of mandate and weak accountability.

Another challenge is the so-called 'fourth sector of development cooperation'[54]. This term refers to non-traditional and non-specialised development players such as hospitals, companies, trade unions, foundations, local authorities (cities and municipalities) as well as countless individual initiatives. Peculiar to most of these initiatives is that a very direct bond is created between people and institutions from the North with people and institutions in the South without institutional middlemen. The growing success of the fourth sector is due on the one hand to an increasing accessibility between North and South (the possibilities of the internet and e-mail, and the increasing number of people who travel to third world countries), and on the other hand to a continuing mistrust of how funds are allocated by state agencies and NGOs ("is the money going where it's needed?). Many state agencies and NGOs in the North, and in the South as well, put a lot of effort into developing their capacity, with the target group itself only being affected indirectly. Visually and emotionally, however, it is the target group who appeals to the average citizen.

Although we would be doing an injustice to the many attempts by development workers to increase professionalism in their sector and to get their supporters directly involved with the South at the same time, it does seem very much that the world of development work is a prisoner of its own logic. That logic states that only one's own organisation can approach 'our people in the South' directly and in a sufficiently legitimate way. This approach has a jovial tint, but is also tainted with exclusivity. What is more, it is determined by a somewhat axiomatic understanding of the equality principle that results in a blind spot towards exploring the intercultural aspect of the partnership. In *Antropologie et développement,* Jean-Paul Olivier de Sardan[55] sketches the prevailing stereotypes: the consensual village community, the 'paysan petit entrepreneur' (peasant turned entrepreneur), the traditional villager, the subordinated villager and the rebellious villager. The development discourse, he says, has all the trademarks of *populism* in the moral sense: we're doing it for the (misunderstood) people. Populism can sound positive ('the people have so much to offer'), which in practice takes the form of grass roots politics (typical of community development). But it may also be a *form of miserablism* ('the poor people who deserve so much better'), which leads to development workers seeing themselves as an avant-garde and directing their efforts at marginal or rebelling sectors (slums, resistance movements). All this occurs when a development worker goes to the South with stereotypical images in mind. In itself, this is only possible if cultural specificity and diversity are denied and the South is defined (from within an ideologically-based mission) through its relationship with the North.

Attention to interculturalism still has far to go in the world of development cooperation. And yet there have been attempts to take the fact of culture seriously both in terms of the partner relationship and in the way that 'development workers' function.

In an article in the professional journal *Coopérer aujourd'hui*[56] published by GRET, it is claimed that the interpretation of the other's values and attitudes occurs mainly implicitly between partners in the North and South. This would seem to be a taboo area, where making differences in values and attitudes (i.e. cultures) more explicit would prove uncomfortable for both parties and, in any case, irrelevant. It also seems that the staff of NGOs are assumed automatically to have the understanding and skills to deal with cultural differences. Philippe Lavigne Delville, one of the article's two authors, emphasises that in an honest analysis of North-South partnerships, the inherent asymmetry of these relationships must be taken into account. The appealing term 'partnership' often conceals a great diversity of institutional relationships that are all too often out of balance: capital often flows in one direction, which inevitably influences authority over the so-called 'joint project'; projects are often short-term and are more significant to some of the organisations involved than others, and the cultures may be very different, whether in terms of national culture, professional culture or organisational culture.

These are all reasons that may lead to a joint project only producing moderate results, or failing completely.

So what can be done? In a system of shared responsibilities, it is unsuitable for certain methods of management to be implicitly attributed to the other partner. And there is no 'one best way' either to estimate the impact of the other's national culture on the organisational culture. This is bound to differ from one continent, region and even country to another. Besides, it does not help, in the absence of a specific policy on interculturalism, for an NGO to rely entirely on the open minds and competence of its staff: a conscientious study of the specific intercultural context, constructing an institutional memory around this, taking it into account when recruiting staff and offering it as an issue in training, would seem to be the minimum that a development organisation can do.

Sylvie Chevrier, the other of the two co-authors, investigates how intercultural management actually takes place in development practice. The most traditional (and still the most common) scenario is for a modest silence to be maintained with respect to cultural differences. These differences are *minimised,* rather than being placed in the spotlight, which may provoke conflicts. The personnel involved indicate – sometimes without really saying as much – that 'sub-optimisation' is acceptable, and confrontation (or anything that could lead to it) is 'not done'. The prevailing attitude is one of *exoticism* (called 'openness' in the world of development work), in the sense that people are supposed to value the other partner's culture systematically. Anyone joining an intercultural team signs a psychological contract: the chance to be enriched by cultural differences implies an attitude of tolerance and an ability to adapt. This often leads to frustrations and a search for release valves (e.g. in breaks during meetings, one can observe people of the same nationality seeking each other out in order to be able to speak 'freely'). It is true that projects handled in this way can be constructive and result-oriented, but this depends completely on the skills and experience of the people involved and the stability of the team. In such cases, staff changes – a matter of course in the world of development work – are damaging for a carefully constructed modus vivendi that is entirely dependent on the individuals involved. Projects become less dependent on individuals when there is a certain amount of recourse to a common professional culture (e.g. two engineers working together on a water collection project) or a common organisational culture. Some NGOs attempt to achieve this by creating a kind of global network with their partners and bringing staff from Southern partners to the North. Although this can certainly bear fruit, studies by Hofstede and others have demonstrated sufficiently that national cultures cannot be neutralised by a common organisational culture. Words, arrangements and working tools continue to have a different meaning, and hence are dealt with differently in practice. What is more, strategies to overcome cultural differences are to a great extent culturally determined in themselves: referring to a professional culture is typically French; the 'cards on the table' way of making unspoken implications explicit is an American approach that may shock Asians. Simply confronting partners with each other's culture can lead to polarisation without progress. This is why Chevrier pleads for a pragmatic and contingent approach. Common practices for action can be sought in different systems of meaning. The type of compromise sought here is not defined in advance: it is partly directed by the situation in itself and by working principles negotiated by the partners. Moreover, it is best if this negotiation can leave sufficient doors open for a culture-specific solution to the arrangements made.

On the basis of a case study, Sarah Mukasa[57] debates the pertinence of employing development workers. In itself this is not new, but in the past this discussion was mainly approached in terms of its cost. Besides structural problems (rapid staff turnover among development workers and undervaluing of the capacities of local staff, different working conditions for ex-pats and local staff for the same work etc.), this study also indicates a lack of cultural understanding as the reason why projects fail. Development workers do not always make the right decisions on sensitive gender and community issues (e.g. who should conduct an interview on the position of widows with respect to land ownership). It can also occur that in a 'particularist' setting where professional and private life blur into each other, certain customs (such as keeping pets) can lead to irritation among local staff. Musaka concludes that NGOs need to pay more attention to the management of development workers, both in the way they are put to work, hierarchic relationships and also cultural sensitivity.

Interculturalism for everyone

We have already discussed the challenge that interculturalism poses to businesses and development organisations. One might conclude that this makes interculturalism a *professional skill*, a chapter to be added to the curriculum of a given subject area. Given the necessary adaptations, this specialist knowledge could also be useful to people in other areas of professional life: politicians, civil servants working for international institutions, scientists, church leaders, journalists and so on.

At the same time, however, interculturalism is becoming more generally accessible as an area of knowledge and experience. In theory anyone might find themselves involved with it. There is of course the increase in *global tourism* that has come a long way since the days of palm beaches, safari parks and mountain treks. Other cultures have become the subject of interest as well: village markets, intercultural dance evenings or tours of favelas and shantytowns. It seems fair to assume that this ever-increasing influx of tourists hardly go unnoticed by local populations. Intentionally or not, a tourist will contribute to a certain image of Western, American, French culture etc. Some travel organisers who consider their business to be 'sustainable tourism' do pay attention to the impressions that Westerners both give and receive at their tropical destination[58].

The movement of people in the opposite direction has a far greater impact. We are talking here about a steadily increasing wave of immigration to the West. This wave of immigration began at the time when many countries were being decolonised, when many Western countries also ex-perienced a demand for unskilled labour. Now, almost 50 years later, 10 to 15% of the population in the West is made up of people of foreign origin. This proportion is bound to increase further, thanks to continuing immigration (refu-gees from areas hit by poverty and war) and higher birth rates among most immigrant groups. Many now belong to the second or third generation and have the official nation-ality of the country where they live. However culture can-not simply be changed like a passport. Besides the question of who is responsible, we cannot get away from the fact that a variety of cultures is experienced as problematic in educa-tion, the workplace and public life. There is no other option for policy than to react to this.

We have seen a certain evolution in policy-making re-sponses. To simplify matters, one could say that for a long time the Western governments turned a blind eye to prob-lems that arose, such as the degeneration of areas with a high immigrant population and racist harassment by the indigenous population. For example, as late as the 1970s, discotheques all over Europe were not even ashamed to hang a sign at the door saying 'no North Africans admit-ted'. The following phase was *target group policy*: migrants were approached as a population group and strengthened with a view to providing better opportunities in education, employment and the community. The results of this policy have not been spectacular, at least not yet. This is why a *policy of diversity* now tends to be preferred. Particularly in the workplace (which is often seen as a driving force for in-tegration), companies are encouraged to work on diversity management: a conscious and strategic approach to allow various groups in society in terms of gender, age or ethnic origin to gain their rightful place in the workplace. Diversity is presented as an asset: improved access to certain markets, a wider range of skills, a better image. However, the question is whether companies can be persuaded to implement such policies. This is not a measure that can be imposed, because it would conflict with an institution seen as important in our society: free enterprise. This also means the freedom to choose whom to recruit or fire.

Interculturalism goes a step further than diversity, even to the extent that it cannot be the direct subject of a policy measure. We defined interculturalism at the beginning of this text as people originating from different cultures working together (on projects, training courses, artistic expression). This could mean, for example, that a company not only employs people from different cultural groups, but that people from these groups spontaneously interact in their daily activities (working, eating, travelling etc.). The question is the extent to which this can be stimulated, or whether it is still a marginal phenomenon, only applicable to a few persons who bridge the gap and to well-defined cultural manifestations such as sport. It may be that interculturalism occurs as a mathematic limit: always to be approached but never to be reached. Perhaps it is realistic to assume that regular 'spontaneous interaction' will only occur when the two or more cultures concerned have changed in themselves, to the point where their basic values no longer differ. But as we have discussed, cultural change is slow.

So it is better to extend the concept of interculturalism to include attempts to work towards it[59].

An important and energising phenomenon that goes hand in hand with interculturalism is its *reflective effect*. Confrontation with another culture teaches people to get to know their own culture. Long-term confrontation enables people to question their own value systems. Peculiar to our time is the confrontation – which some would call a conflict – between Western and Islamic culture. These labels alone hint at a certain asymmetry: on the one hand, a society whose base note is economic, and on the other a society with religious foundations. There is one major similarity: both are expansive systems. Western economy, markets, products and advertising are forcing their way uninvited into the furthest outreaches of the world. Islam has the ambition, at least, to convert non-Muslims to 'the true belief'. Confrontation in the form of conflict can entrench both systems, convincing each that they are right. But peaceful confrontation can be an eye-opener, questioning what has been taken for granted, learning to understand differences. Why shouldn't Muslim women be allowed to study or look for work? Or why is it self-evident that you shouldn't copy pop music, that naked bodies on huge posters should be used to advertise a brand of watches or that Western countries can export their rubbish to poor African countries [60]? Who can claim to overcome the particularities of his or her own cultural setting when judging the other?

This brings us back to the debate on cultural relativism and Levinas' responses: one can legitimately look beyond cultures when one does so together with the other. The advantage of cultural relativism is that one does not consider one's own culture to be the ultimate truth. The disadvantage is that people close themselves off from other cultures in moral indifference. Dialogue is the only way out of this deadlock. If dialogue is impossible, frustration grows, along with a feeling of 'us-and-them' and the cultural divide. There is no way to ask 'why?' if malicious spyware finds its way onto our computer, no way of negotiating with suicide bombers and no way to ask anonymous capital speculators to be reasonable.

Levinas and his philosophy have a prominent place in the curricula of training courses on interculturalism for adult professionals (NGO workers and businesspeople, immigrants and migration workers, as well as a wider audience of interested people). A typical curriculum would probably feature introductions from the perspective of anthropology and moral philosophy, areas of common ground with other subject areas and social sectors, with approaches to aspects of their disciplines (religions, politics, environment, intercultural communication and policies of diversity, diplomacy and law, health care and aid, economic relations and development work). It also may include area studies on the major continents with in-depth studies of certain issues. Programmes like these, as well as short workshops and individual lectures tend to be very popular..Their success does demonstrate that the wider public increasingly shows a well-intentioned interest in interculturalism.

The coconut allegory

We would like to offer a short excursus here, sketching an example of how interculturalism can be taught simply to target groups who may not have an academic background. The Living Stone Center[61], a knowledge centre with its roots in the tourist sector, offers intercultural encounter tours to specific target groups in the business community and the non profit sector. In its accompanying training package, the Living Stone Center uses its 'coconut model' as a metaphor with an educational explanatory purpose. Coconuts are found in many countries, have positive connotations (nutrition, raw material, fuel) and have different layers. Their layered nature is used to illustrate the 'layers' of a culture.

From the outside working inwards, we encounter the following layers:
- the outermost layer is the smooth rind: the visual reality of a culture (its architecture, gastronomy, greetings and etiquette, language etc.)
- beneath that is a fibrous layer: its systems and institutions (that determine how people interact, both in private and in public)
- beneath that is a hard shell that separates the visible and tangible from the invisible (symbols such as the cross, Tibetan prayer flags in a landscape etc.)
- then we come to the flesh, the invisible but known heart of a culture (its norms, values, conventions and beliefs)
- finally, we have the very centre, the liquid coconut milk (the often subconscious basic assumptions that deter-

mine the position of human beings with respect to time, nature and other people).

This innermost layer is difficult to grasp, a fact symbolised by its liquid state. It can only be perceived indirectly (using patterns of answers to statements or dilemmas, like those developed by Hofstede and Trompenaars). These basic assumptions can also be described conceptually as particularist or universalist, masculine or feminine, short-term or long-term oriented etc.

An insight into this complex system of layers is only a first step in a process of gradually increasing involvement. Insight is preceded by a phase of interest, which is followed in turn by the removal of a defensive attitude. Insight then leads – still according to the educational model – to the state where one values the other culture, learning to see through the other's eyes. This in turn leads to the final step: internalising a positive communicative attitude with respect to other cultures, which is reflected in behaviour and life choices.

Clearly the above is a very schematic description of a process that takes place in practice in fits and starts, with obstacles and areas of incompleteness. Furthermore, remaining within the allegory, one can say: you don't need to eat the whole coconut all at once to get a taste for it.

...

This short reflection on the phenomenon of 'interculturalism' has covered a range of subjects and charted several approaches: philosophy, sociology, psychology and practical experience in the field. There is a strong suggestion that cultures do not simply adapt to one another in order to form a 'higher' culture. Insight, respect and the ability to deal with differences seem to be the greatest we are capable of. In our non-exhaustive look at the available bodies of knowledge, we have moreover established that such insight is currently limited. Nonetheless, a minority of people do show an increasing will to learn more. This is linked to the will, likewise increasing, to interact with people from other cultures. Cultural differences, as we have seen, are deeply entrenched, tenacious, and important. They can be described but not completely explained, just like life itself. Yet cultures are not frozen skeletons of extinct species. They are as much alive as the people who live within them. This means that for intercultural communication now and in the future, there is no reason for pessimism.

NOTES

1. M. van der Goes van Naters was a 20th century Dutch politician. The quote comes from his auto-biographical work published in 1980: *Met en tegen de tijd. Herinneringen (With and against the Time. Memories)*.
2. Raymond Williams (1976), *Keywords,* London: Fontana.
3. Kroeber A. & Kluckhorn C. (1952), *Culture*, New York: Meridian Books, p.181.
4. UNESCO (1982), *World Conference on Cultural Policies*, Mexico City.
5. Put in Marxist terms, culture is opposed to structure, on the implicit assumption that it is structure (i.e. modes of production) that determines

culture. Terms used in this context (again implying causality) are infrastructure and superstructure.

6. In people's experience these aspects will dominate if you ask about their culture: a number of values and the feeling of belonging to the group that adheres to these values.

7. It was important to pay tribute to cultural relativism in order at least to question the assumption of Western superiority. But the cultural relativist propaganda of 'respect' can also be seen as a form of indifference: a reason – or an excuse – not to have to intervene in injustices far from our back yard. Feminism, a product of the West, hesitated for a long time over the question of whether it could approach 'other civilisations'. Cultural relativism also provided an easy way out for dictators and authoritarian regimes (e.g. Mobutu who declared that there was no place for democracy in the culture of Zaire at the time; the USSR that consistently rejected any reference to human rights as 'unjustifiable meddling in domestic affairs' and so on).

8. Galton has been called the father of the eugenics movement, a philosophy that reacted against the mixing of races and that was partially put into practice in certain Northern countries (USA, Canada, Scandinavia and also Nazi Germany) in the form of forcible sterilizations of socially weak groups and mentally handicapped people. What has remained in the popular discourse on culture and still raises its head mainly in situations of conflict, is the tendency to think in terms of superior and inferior cultures.

9. Lévi-Strauss C. (1947), *Structures élémentaires de la parenté,* Paris: Presses Univ.

10. Particular to a dialectic reading of history is the cyclical movement "external stimulus – basic idea – development – decay (alienation from the basic idea) and ultimate catharsis". The decay stage is universally applicable. The internet, for example, was born (in the academic world) from the need to exchange scientific data more quickly. It has evolved into a 'source' of data on just about everything (including music releases, porn and the dissemination of terror). Decay is also present in the fact that the content of the information (its validity and reliability) is becoming dubious. Catharsis can lead either to revolution, reform or reconciliation with the reality that formed the external impetus for the basic idea (in our example reform, i.e. the introduction of systems to ensure reliability, would seem to be the most probable way out). This reconciliation is understood in the sense of a 'step

forward,' because one has been strengthened by the experience (in our case, 'reconciliation' might mean that the general accessibility of the internet is removed, in exchange for specialised electronic communication systems). The triad of thesis-antithesis-synthesis gives an incorrect image of dialectics, as though synthesis were a sort of 'compromise' between thesis and antithesis. In fact the synthesis is the same as the thesis (the basic idea), but enriched by the (negative) experience of the antithesis.

11. Among Girard's most important books are *La violence et le sacré* (1972), *Le bouc émissaire* (1982) and *Des choses cachées depuis la fondation du monde* (1983).

12. In his most recent work, *Les origines de la culture* (2004), Girard returns again to his central concept: mimetic desire. This is what distinguishes us from animals and enables us to construct our own identities. We use imitation to learn everything we need to take part in society by means of adaptation to it. We are so conditioned in this imitative behaviour from early childhood that we continue with it all our lives as a survival mechanism. Nonetheless, mimetic desire is not predestined, but rather derives from a certain freedom of action that leads to the choice of a certain form (model). Religion, for Girard, is a phenomenon that on the one hand justifies the sequence of this mimesis (desire – rivalry – crisis – sacrifice), but on the other hand prevents violence. One might think that Girard's theory of culture cannot be generalised because he – himself a practising Christian – sees an evolution in Christianity that can break through the succession of mimesis (culture) and the crisis of sacrifice (violence) in the long term. Just like Darwin in the natural sciences, Girard believes in an evolutionary progress that can go beyond this compulsive repetition.

13. Levinas E. (1961), *Totalité et Infini*, the Hague : Martinus Nijhoff.

14. Logical positivism is the reigning model for science. Conclusions are not drawn from convictions or reasoning (which one can agree or disagree with), but demonstrable facts. This demonstrability means that the scientist makes an empirical selection and, if necessary, carries out an experiment (such as a standardised survey) in such a way that it can be reproduced by another, independent scientist.

15. In more general terms: it is inappropriate to ascribe group characteristics (gender, race, class, age group, etc.) to an individual without knowing this individual. To do so is to be guilty of prejudice.

16. Benedict R. (1946), *The Chrysanthenum and the Sword*, Boston: Houghton.
17. Hall E.T. (1959), *The Silent Language*, New York: Achor Books; *The Hidden Dimension (1969)*, New York: Achor Books
18. Geert Hofstede & Gert Jan Hofstede (1991), *Cultures and Organisations: Software of the Mind. Intercultural Cooperation and Its Importance for Survival*, New York: McGraw-Hill. The IBM-survey is described at full length in Hofstede's former major book, *Culture's Consequences* (1980).
19. This contradicts an often-held traditional belief that the Germans are loyal to figures in authority. It may be proof that German culture has radically changed since 1945 and that the stereotypes are lagging behind reality.
20. 'It is not because Jove is entitled to something that an ox also has this right'
21. 'Agreements are binding'.
22. Both long-term and short-term oriented cultures contain Confucian elements, the 'investment in later' and the 'respect for tradition' respectively. This means that both the traditional nature of old China up to 1940 and its current accelerated growth can therefore be explained from a Confucian background.
23. According to Hofstede, Brazil's high score may be linked to the presence of a Japanese minority there.
24. This matrix is not taken from Hofstede's book. Our intention is merely to show how Hofstede's theory can make the phenomenon of national culture practically applicable in education studies, politics and business.
25. Henry Mintzberg is generally considered to be an important authority in the field of management and organisations. His most famous works are *The Nature of Managerial Work* (1973), *The Structuring of Organisations* (1979) and – the work to which Hofstede refers – *Structure in Fives: Designing Effective Organizations* (1983).
26. Hofstede only measures the direction of the attitude (for or against) and not its strength (how important is it to people?) or crystallisation (did this attitude exist before questions were asked about it?).
27. Trompenaars, F. & C. Hampden-Turner (1993), *Riding the Waves of Culture: Understanding Diversity in Global Business*, New York: McGraw-Hill.
28. Trompenaars F. and P. Woolliams (2003), *Business across Cultures*, London: Capstone Publications.

29. Parsons, Talcott, and Edward Shills (Eds.). (1951). *Toward a General Theory of Action*. Cambridge: Harvard University Press.
30. Hoogvelt, A. (1976), *The Sociology of Developing Societies*, London: McMillan.
31. Kluckhohn, F.R. and F.L. Strodtbeck (1961), *Variations in value orientations*. Row, Peterson & Company, New York.
32. A summary of these can be found, for example, in Dahl S. (2000), *Communications and Culture Transformation:: Cultural Diversity, Globalization and Cultural Convergence*, London: ECE.
33. Schwartz is a social psychologist working at the University of Jerusalem. His most important publication for our purposes is: Schwartz, S. & L. Sagiv (1995), Identifying Culture-Specifics in the Content and Structure of Values. *Journal of Cross Cultural Psychology*, n° 26, pp. 92-116.
34. Schwartz was indeed mainly concerned with European countries.
35. Inglehart R. (1977), *The silent revolution. Changing values and political styles among Western publics*, Princeton: University Press.
36. A summary of this and other systems of value orientations can be found in: De Witte H., Ideological Orientations and Values, *Encyclopedia of Applied Psychology*, Volume X, Elsevier Publications.
37. Giddens A.(1993), *Sociology*, 2nd ed. Cambridge: Polity Press, p.57
38. Robertson R. (1992), *Globalization*, London: Sage
39. Huntington S. (1996), *The Clash of Civilisations,* New York: Simon & Schuster; Harrison LE & Huntington S. (eds) (2000), *Culture matters*, New York: Basic Books.
40. Harvey D. (1989), *The Condition of Postmodernity*, Oxford: Blackwell.
41. Castells M. (1996.1997.1998), *The Information Age,* Malden: Blackwell.
42. As shown, application (by M.H. Bond) of Hofstede's research in China and other East Asian countries has produced a fifth cultural dimension (short-term versus long-term orientation) alongside the original four. At the end of the 1990s, a similar study was launched in a number of African countries (with a control group of European and Asian countries, and a total of 1120 respondents spread over 14 countries). However this study did not reveal any new dimensions, and neither did it allow African countries to be distinguished from each other, with the exception of certain colonial 'inheritances'. (Noorderhaven N. & B. Tidjani, Culture, Governance and Economic Perfor-

mance: An Explorative Study with a Special Focus on Africa, in *International Journal of Cross Cultural Management*, 2001 Vol 1(1), pp.31-52.)

43. Luhmann N. (1991), *Soziale Systeme. Grundriss einer algemeine Theorie*, Suhrkamp, p.224.

44. Are cultures social systems in themselves? According to the system theory, social systems are in essence reducers of complexity, and this is what distinguishes them from their surroundings. The understanding of cultures as complex systems would offer an explanation for their cyclical nature (with a rise and fall, just like other complex systems such as weather and climate types or economies). Simple systems, in contrast, such as meetings, car journeys or the fall of a meteorite, are linear and determined by time. A reading of cultures from system theory would also reveal the cyclical nature of a specific culture: when people cherish their culture (e.g. creating living museums such as the Black Country Museum (UK), organising cultural weeks etc.) rather than carrying out the activities that make the culture itself (farming for oneself, making music oneself etc.) then the culture is no longer producing and ordering on its own behalf ('autopoiesis') but becomes self-referential (its own aim). The seed is no longer sown but eaten: this could be the indication of cultural decline. The reasoning we have followed here is not typical of system theory, however, which – complex in itself and directed at complexity – prefers to look through revealing, but static, lenses. Culture cannot be 'seen' through this type of lens.

45. One might ask whether culture and ethnic characteristics are not linked in the notion of 'temperament' (which is said to be reflected in individuals' physiological and mental characteristics). To go into this is beyond the scope of this article. Given the ease with which people resort to prejudices, we would advise caution when making claims about a possible genetic basis for certain group characteristics. However a taboo in social science circles is hypocritical if one considers that genetic research in biomedical sciences is more prominent than ever before. This genetic research includes research into all kinds of 'social' characteristics such as sexual preferences, alcoholism or violent behaviour. Biomedical genetic research justifies itself by presenting the prospect of rapid practical applications.

46. Adler, P. (1975). The transitional experience: An alternative view of cultural shock. *Journal of Humanistic Psychology*, *15*, 13-23.

47. Milton Bennett (1986), A developmental approach to training for inter-cultural sensitivity, *International Journal of Intercultural Relations* 10(2), pp.179-195).

48. Black J.S. & M. Mendenhall (1990), Cross-Cultural Training Effectiveness: A Review and Theoretical Framework for Future Research. *Academy of Management Review*, 15(1), pp.113-136. Mendenhall is a co-founder and partner of the Kozai Group, a consultancy bureau based in St. Louis (USA) that deals with international HRM and expatriates management.

49. Harrison J.K (1994)., Developing successful expatriate managers: a framework for the structural design and strategic alignment of cross-cultural training programs, Human Resource Planning, 17(3), pp.17-35.

50. www.sietar.org

51. www.itapintl.com

52. Structural aid is the opposite of emergency aid. Structural aid is intended to be preventative ("don't give them fish but teach them how to fish") and takes the form of community development and support of poorer groups who are becoming organised. A proportion of structural aid is explicitly political: local organisations or movements are given financial assistance with the intention that they become able to act as a countervailing power to corrupt local regimes or to the economic interests of the North.

53. Roberts S.M., J.P. Jones & O. Fröhling (2005), NGOs and the Globalization of Managerialism : A Research Framework, in *World Development*, 33 (11), pp.1845-1864. The best-known knowledge centre for the functioning of NGOs is probably INTRAC (International NGO Training and Research Center).

54. Develtere P. (2005), De Belgische Ontwikkelingssamenwerking, Leuven: Davidsfonds. The 'fourth sector' of development players includes all players who are not part of the first three domain-specific sectors (i.e. bilateral, multilateral or indirect aid, or in other words: the governmental donor agencies, international institutions and NGOs).

55. Olivier de Sardan J.P. (1997), Anthropologie et développement. Essai en socio-anthropologie de développement social, Paris : Karthala.

56. Chevrier S. & P Lavigne Delville (2005), Les enjeux du management inter-culturel dans les projets de coopération au développement. Une question sous-estimée ? *Coopérer aujourd'hui* n°44, Paris: GRET (Groupe de recherche et d'échanges technologiques).

57. Mukasa S.(1999), *Are expatriate staff necessary in international development NGOs? A case study in an international NGO in Uganda*, CVO International Working Paper 4, Centre for Civil Society, London School of Economics.

58. This is another area where we have observed a tendency towards subject specialisation. At Berkeley University, an interdisciplinary Tourism Studies Working Group was founded in 2003 (www.tourismstudies.org). Several years before that, Sheffield Hallam University had already inaugurated a Centre for Tourism and Culture Change (www.tourism-culture.com). Both institutes mainly offer training packages and academic events (conferences).

59. This low common denominator could also include cultural management. W.A. Shadid sees intercultural management as the measures taken (1) to promote the participation of groups in the company, (2) to recognise the cultural diversity of staff at individual and group level and (3) to promote mutual acceptance in the workplace. Shadid W.A. (1998), *Fundamentals of Intercultural Communication*, The Hague: Kluwer.

60. Inherent to the classification of Western society as economic, with capital dominating over the other production factors (labour and natural resources) is the 'commodification' of human beings and objects, where 'everything has a price' is part of the culture. In Marxist terms, this is the stage where the exchange value of goods (or human effort) no longer corresponds to their utility value. In a following stage, buying and selling in themselves become an aspect of culture, without reference to the utility value of objects. The prices of raw material markets are determined to a great extent here by speculation (i.e. estimates of the price that the same goods can be bought or sold for in the future). In other words, buyers do not need the raw materials themselves. Nonetheless, even small increases or decreases in these prices can mean the difference between getting by and bitter poverty for the producers of these materials (in areas of Africa or Latin America). Hence culture can never be seen as independent of economic relationships.

61. Full name: Living Stone – Centre for Intercultural Sustainable Enterprise. The two main stakeholders are Joker Travel and the Catholic University of Leuven. See: www.lscoop.com

The Intercultural Momentum

What the South says: a survey

IGNACE POLLET,
PATRICK DEVELTERE

The Intercultural Momentum
What the South says: a survey

The aim: a poll based on discernement and experience

Before, during and after: dealing with time

Nothing personal, only business – or is it?

Negotiations and consensus

Differences in leadership

Opening to the other culture

Who thinks what? Types among perception

Image and reality

In this third part of this publication we bring the voice from the South into the story by means of a survey. There are good reasons for doing so. Most sociologists and economists view North-South relationships in terms of either financial interests, or (whether conflicting or not) different systems of values. They are looking into the cultural foundations for lower productivity or the creation of welfare[1]. This is a macro-approach, which often takes place on the basis of purely deductive grounds[2]. Authors such as Hofstede[3] and Schwartz[4] may produce a very broad empirical database, but their findings concern primarily cultural systems and dimensions. Only rarely (is there even one example?) is the intercultural momentum examined: what happens when people from North and South find themselves in the same boat, come across each other at a meeting, establish a project together or meet just once? This intercultural momentum takes place at a micro-level. By deploying a survey, we aim to go beyond the pure anecdotal. Above all we choose explicitly – with all the limitations that a survey has – to let people from the South to talk and to give an interpretation as to what happens during an intercultural meeting. To start with, we briefly cover the method used in the collection of data. Subsequently the most striking results are presented. We conclude by elucidating the relevance of this survey in conjunction with current views and the possible areas of knowledge expansion in the future.

The aim: a poll based on discernment and experience

All good things consist of three parts, so does the study of social sciences. Consequently, apart from a theoretical introduction ("Same world, different paths") and a practical methodology ("The world in a coconut"), one must not ignore the empirical component in the triptych. We thus focused our attention on intercultural meetings in professional practices and the respective impressions of those involved from the South, which underline their own behavioural pattern and perception as much as those of the people from the North. We wanted to zoom in on this intercultural 'momentum' in a manner which would yield less hasty and more personal material. That is why a survey seemed the obvious thing to do. Because of the purely explorative and speculative character of this research exercise we chose a survey made with low sample numbers and non-representative random sampling. Representation is a difficult requirement if one has as a starting point that the population is 'the population of the South'. Therefore it was decided to carry out the survey via email with consultants, researchers and other professional points of contact situated in the South (Africa, Asia and Latin America) with which the research team of the Living Stone has had professional contact in the last five years. Participants had to fulfil certain criteria such as: they must have been brought up and live in the South, they must not be European but must have (had) professional contact with Europeans. Hence because of practical considerations the object of the survey was narrowed to people from the South professionally dealing with Europeans. We are well aware that inter-culturality is a factor in the non-professional environment, that Europeans do not represent the only 'different culture' (for example an Indian, a Kenyan and a Nigerian represent a different culture for a Senegalese) and that Europeans as 'culture' do not form a homogeneous club. There are practical reasons also for the latter: the survey had to be kept brief so there was no option to be specific for experiences with British, French, Germans etc. On the other hand 'the North' and 'the West' are too vague terms, or they carry a specific connotation. Although the remark was often made that there are differences between European nationalitites, the respondents showed insight by basing their answers on a sort of imaginary average.

The questionnaire itself consists of a series of statements (38 in total) where the respondents must choose their answer according to the Lickert-scale (a scale of 5: totally agreeing, mostly agreeing, neither agreeing or disagreeing, mostly disagreeing and totally disagreeing)[5]. The survey was carried out in the second half of 2006 and produced a total response of 106 valid, complete questionnaires[6].

A first look at the response showed us the following: out of the 106 respondents 57 come from Africa, 25 from Asia and 24 from Latin America. When comparing the three continents the 5 respondents from North Africa (Egypt and Morocco) and West Asia (Iran) are not included because of their considerably different culture from the continents of which they form a geophysical part.

135

74 of the respondents are men, 32 are women. In terms of age we have 20 in their 20's, 34 in their 30's, 24 in their 40's and 28 are over 50. The professional distribution is as follows: 12 are businessmen (self-employed or in the higher employment sector), 37 work in the NGO sector, 41 are academics or consultants and 16 work for the government or are employees. Another identification question was how frequent were their contacts with Europeans. 43 mention continuous professional contact (daily), 46 have reasonably to very frequent contact (at least monthly to at least weekly) while 17 have only occasional contact with Europeans (annually or less than every 12 months).

We pooled the results of the survey around the following themes: dealing with time; distinction between the personal and the professional; how one reaches decisions; interpretation of leadership; respect for local traditions and cultural openness; types in terms of perception. By presenting numerical data we shall from time to time refer to differences in perception between Africans, Asians and Latin Americans. It must also be noted that the respondents from North Africa and the Middle East have not been assigned to Africa and Asia respectively. Their absolute number (5) is actually too low to justify a separate category.

The presented numbers mirror perceptions. Perceptions are realities, often themselves important realities because one attaches to them behaviour and expected behaviour. At the same time perceptions are often unreliable or deformations of the reality to which they refer. They can be based on one's own experiences as well as on discernment and hearsay. One's own experiences may have been, by co-incidence, positive or negative. Hence we ask the reader to interpret such results with the appropriate caution.

Before, during and after: dealing with time

A number of questions aimed towards the perception of behaviour of Europeans and of own compatriots in connection with:
- to inform beforehand that a meeting is to take place;
- preparation for a meeting;
- how quickly one arrives 'to the point';
- how quickly one demands results;
- regarding a meeting as a step in a longer process.

According to our respondents from the South, Europeans appear to announce a meeting well in advance and be well prepared contrary to their own compatriots:

Perception of all respondents	Europeans usually let us know long enough in advance when they want to have a meeting	People from my country usually let their foreign partners know long enough in advance when they want to have a meeting.
Agree	90.6	35.8
In between	6.6	25.5
Disagree	2.8	38.7
Total	100.0	100.0

Perception of all respondents	Europeans usually come to a meeting well prepared.	People from my country usually come to a meeting well prepared.
Agree	87.7	48.1
In between	10.4	23.6
Disagree	1.9	28.3
Total	100.0	100.0

Europeans have also a different use of time during the meeting: they want to wrap up faster than people from the South. Apart from that, the people from the South take more time than Europeans to listen to those with whom they are dealing:

Perception of all respondents	Europeans tend to come to the point very quickly.	People from my country tend to come to the point very quickly.
Agree	82.1	22.6
In between	11.3	24.5
Disagree	6.6	52.8
Total	100.0	100.0

Perception of all respondents	Europeans tend to take the necessary time to listen to what we have to say.	People from my country tend to take the necessary time to listen to what their European partners have to say.
Agree	70.8	81.1
In between	18.9	14.2
Disagree	10.4	4.7
Total	100.0	100.0

Above all Europeans want a meeting to produce results more than the people from the South, for they consider the meeting to be more like a step in a longer process:

Perception of all respondents	Europeans usually want very quick results from a joint-undertaking.	People from my country usually want very quick results from a joint-undertaking
Agree	75.5	54.7
In between	12.3	28.3
Disagree	12.3	17.0
Total	100.0	100.0

Perception of all respondents	Europeans see a meeting just as a meeting and not as a step in a long-lasting relationship	People from my country see a meeting just as a meeting and not as a step in a long-lasting relationship.
Agree	52.8	25.5
In between	25.5	14.1
Disagree	21.7	60.4
Total	100.0	100.0

As people from the South see it, the emphasis in time management for Europeans lies on "before": one plans well in advance, so that the meeting will proceed faster and with no surprises. Above all Europeans work towards results: a meeting is an investment that must deliver. With people from the South the emphasis lies on 'during' and also on the timeless: we are partners, therefore it is important that we listen a lot to each other. A meeting is not an investment but a constituent part of a process. If one engages in a partnership, it is not for a short while – as we shall see in the following paragraph.

These differences regarding time perspective can lead to misunderstandings and be a source of aggravation. Europeans attending a meeting in Africa observe that the planning is only made when everyone is around the table. This has practical reasons. The context has many contingencies which cannot be foreseen in advance: who is going to be present? Who is stuck in an airport? Will the equipment work? But there is also another fundamental, culturally determined reason: first see with whom we sit around the table, first learn about each other sufficiently, so one thinks in Africa, then we can do business. Africans, but also Latin Americans, are inclined to announce formally a simple intervention in a conference with the appropriate attention, formalities and placements. The fact that this requires much (expensive) time is taken into account. These cultural differences may be explained by several of the Hofstede's dimensions (dealing with insecurity and short/long term focusing). Trompenaars attributes the emphasis that people in the South put on the 'now' to the dichotomy between sequential cultures and concurrent cultures. In the trail of Hall one may suggest that for many people from the South a meeting is a 'low context' moment in a culture which is essentially 'high context'. Hence the inclination to explicitly deal with each detail, out of fear of making 'a mistake'.

Away from the elucidating models, what it comes down to in practice is that one must not try to outdo one another but to be willing to come half way. The difference in time conception is not disconnected from another cultural 'schism' between North and South: universalism and particularism. The following paragraph is dedicated to this.

Nothing personal, only business – or is it?

Social scientists like Parsons[7] and Trompenaars[8] work with dichotomous (being diametrically opposite each other) cultural variables. The characterisation on the basis of universalism *vs* particularism is a striking example. In cultural terms universalism means that one is driven in his acts in all situations and facing all people by the same rules and principles; whereas particularism means that the kind of relation one has with someone determines the ways one handles the other person with. This means concretely that there is a different set of rules, for example, for people of the same group (familial, ethnic, nationality) than for 'outsiders': one borrows or lends with no interest, one closes the eyes in case of breaching of rules, one favours relatives with promotions.

One of the questions in the survey probed the desirability of mixing personal and business interest:

Perception of all respondents	Europeans are eager to get to know us personally	People from my country are eager to get to know their European partners personally.
Agree	52.8	89.6
In between	21.7	3.8
Disagree	25.5	6.6
Total	100.0	100.0

In the South it is very desirable to have a closer personal acquaintance between 'business contacts', much more than for Europeans. 44% of the participants find the fact that

Europeans are not interested in getting acquainted with them as a hindrance to the establishment of connections.

Above all it is assumed by friends that they shall be friends for life. In this sense people from the South are disappointed at the long radio silence from Europe...

Perception of all respondents	Europeans usually keep in touch after they have returned to their country	People from my country usually keep in touch with their European guests after they have returned to their country.
Agree	49.1	73.6
In between	21.7	17.6
Disagree	29.2	8.5
Total	100.0	100.0

In the series 'characteristics of Europeans harmful to setting up ties' 39% of the respondents declared: they do not maintain contact after they have left. This is not the 'biggest sin' of the Europeans, but it shows that duration and sincerity of contacts in the South (primarily Africa) is held in high esteem.

The fact that the personal is clearly important in the South, has extreme implications for intercultural contacts. It is in one's interests to send the same person whenever a European organisation is to establish a partner organisation in the South. Someone that one knows, even better the same person who originally set up the contact. Afterwards one advises, whenever people from the South come to Europe, to invest in the necessary care at the reception, just like Europeans are 'pampered' in the South. That means: picking them up personally from the airport, coming to look for them in the hotel, going out to eat together ... People from the South are often astonished that they are left on their own – while Europeans often prefer to be left in peace.

Perception of all respondents	In a meeting involving people from my country and European partners, people from my country usually show more hospitality than Europeans.
Agree	84.0
In between	12.3
Disagree	3.8
Total	100.0

Another consequence of this 'particularism' is that Europeans show best the necessary restraint in setting up local networks. Because not everyone can or wants to work in that way with everyone:

Perception of all respondents	In my country, most people prefer only to carry out a job with people they know.
Agree	65.1
In between	15.1
Disagree	19.8
Total	100.0

Following the functionalistic sociology, particularism is often looked down upon as 'old fashioned'. But it is a reality in many non-European countries. There are also advantages in getting things done in a context where institutions often function laboriously. Above all particularism is 'of the people' and in this sense something universal: Europeans will also fall back onto their own families, their acquaintances, colleagues or compatriots in times of crises and in uncertain or strange situations.

Negotiations and consensus

In the list 'harmful characteristics of Europeans' (10 statements that one can quote as 'very harmful', 'to some extent harmful', 'occurs but is not harmful' and 'does not occur') this is what it was most often declared as harmful: 'they want us to accept their point of view'. No less than 62.3% of the respondents found this 'very or to some extent harmful'.

Anthropologists know that in many southern countries intense, potentially or effectively conflicting matters are solved through long discussions. Factors, crucial next to the input of time, are: not to make one lose face, the group is more important than the individual (loyalty) and everyone has a say. This last thing is attributed to a simple psychic pattern: through the mere expression (a physical action) of an idea, which one originally did not support, one is inclined to adjust one's own attitude. At the end one reaches an understanding which everybody can live with.

Europeans have certainly broken away from obtaining a solution in that manner. One does not put time into undertaking long-drawn negotiations. Also the loyalty to the group is not taken for granted. In addition losing face is not a point for the Europeans: because of the strict separation between business and personal, Europeans are able to let their negotiating partners fail miserably in public and still pat him or her amicably on the shoulder after the meeting. People from the South, for whom the negotiating process is something personal, do not understand something like this. They often smile politely and meanwhile in silence they conclude that the European in question is not a trustworthy partner, not someone that they can gladly work with.

This came out in our survey, yet the differences are relative – and in this sense they can be bridged over:

Perception of all respondents	Europeans try to persuade us rather than to look for a compromise	People from my country try to persuade their European partners rather than to look for a compromise.
Agree	56.6	39.6
In between	18.9	21.7
Disagree	24.5	38.7
Total	100.0	100.0

There are big differences on this last point (People from my country try to persuade ...) between Africans (24.1% agree), Asians (47.8% agree) and Latin Americans (62.5% agree). This may indicate that Latin Americans do not interpret the dominant attitude of the Europeans as 'taken for granted' as much as the Africans do. They want to stand up at specific moments for when they think 'they are right'.

Next to how one reaches decisions, there is also the general manner of negotiating, the 'style':

Perception of all respondents	Europeans tend to be dominant during meetings.
Agree	54.7
In between	21.7
Disagree	23.6
Total	100.0

147

Again it is Africa (64.8% agree) that feels it most clearly amongst the three continents.

Differences in leadership

Whoever, as European, wants to do business in Africa with an African partner, may think: I must make sure that I deal with the boss and only with the boss. And he must think – even if it is not so in reality – that I am also the boss.

We found that it was worth looking into a number of stereotypes around leadership, because they are perhaps crucial for the success of intercultural undertakings. These stereotypes, which are very popular in Europe, sound like:
- in the South the boss takes all decisions himself, in the North one delegates more;
- in the South the boss is a male, in the North can equally be a female;
- in the South the boss must exercise direct supervision over his subordinates, in the North this is not necessary;
- in the South the boss will not tolerate any objections, in the North he will.

We asked for the perception of our (southern) respondents on each one of these points:

Perception of all respondents	As far as I know, in Europe, a leader of an organization takes the decisions by him(her)self, without delegating it to other staff.	In my country, a leader of an organization takes the decisions by him(her)self, without delegating it to other staff.
Agree	17.0	55.6
In between	39.6	18.9
Disagree	43.4	25.5
Total	100.0	100.0
Perception of all respondents	In Europe, I think women are considered just as suitable as men to take the leadership of an organization.	In my country, women are considered just as suitable as men to take the leadership of an organization.
Agree	76.4	33.0
In between	15.1	15.1
Disagree	8.5	51.9
Total	100.0	100.0
Perception of all respondents	In Europe, I think a boss has to keep an eye on his employees, otherwise they do not work.	In my country, a boss has to keep an eye on his employees, otherwise they do not work.
Agree	21.7	61.3
In between	27.4	17.0
Disagree	50.9	21.7
Total	100.0	100.0
Perception of all respondents	In Europe, it is all right to disagree with a superior.	In my country, it is all right to disagree with a superior.
Agree	55.7	17.9
In between	27.3	17.0
Disagree	17.0	65.1
Total	100.0	100.0

In a certain sense the 'stereotypes' are confirmed in that way. Without tying here any moral judgement, it is at least positive that one is conscious of the consequences of the (possibly relative) differences in interpretation about leadership. In the North one has to be conscious to put the emphasis on chief-to-chief talks for the most important discussions between partner organisations. At the same time it is valid to say that whenever a southern organisation is visited by someone from the North, who is in no position of leadership in his own organisation, there is no implication that this person does not have 'full powers'. To acknowledge and accept differences in forms is a learning process from which all parties involved can benefit.

Political correctness should not prevent us from seeing that in the South the road still needs to be opened for women to be able to be accepted in leading positions. Amongst the three southern continents the Latin Americans consider themselves as the most emancipated one (42% agree that it is acceptable to them to object to their superiors; 54% think that in their country women are as capable as men for leadership).

Opening to the other culture

In the series of questions about 'harmful characteristics' we investigated how the southerners perceive the cultural empathy of the Europeans. Two statements drew our attention:

Characteristic of Europeans	Percentage of respondents finding this very harmful or to some extent harmful
They are offensive in terms of eating or clothing habits	11.3 %
They are not interested in our cultural identity	42.5 %

This implies that Europeans are seen to do their best to adapt but at the same time in many cases there is no sincere interest.

In the last batch of questions the respondents were asked why, according to them, the Europeans, whom they have met in a professional context, actually came here (= the South).

These numbers are harsh at first sight for Europeans: they come here to do their thing, often looking for fast results. At the same time there is positive news: many come here to do something about the poverty[9]. Almost 56% consider Europeans to be genuinely interested in the local culture, while others (46%) suspect that for some this is a sort of exotic 'peeping'.

Perceived motivation and attitude of Europeans	Percentage of respondents finding this greatly true or to some extent true
They are investing and look for making a quick profit	53.7
They are investing and want things to succeed step by step	88.7
They come here as specialists who are looking for a professional success	68.9
They come here out of curiosity; it is a form of tourism	46.2
They come here with a mission of helping the poor	67.9
They come here with a mission of creating ties with a local community	51.9
They are interested to learn about our culture	55.7

Who thinks what? Types concerning perception

We have pointed here and there in the previous paragraphs to the differences in perception between Africans, Asians and Latin Americans. We are aware that the classification of the respondents into 'continental culture groups' does injustice to those who sometimes come from very different national cultures. The respondents had the same reaction when they were asked to comment on the list of questions: there is no such thing as 'the Europeans', was often the spontaneous response. In this sense we need to seriously adjust comments on 'continental groups', particularly in the light of the small number of respondents.

Above all there are reasons as to why we should accept that we could also meet significant differences amongst groups on the basis of sex, profession and the frequency of contact with Europeans.

By looking at the most significant differences, a profile is drawn of the African respondents on a number of areas:
- 65% of the Africans find that Europeans are dominant during meetings (compared to 48% of the Asians and 42% of the Latin Americans);
- only 35% of the Africans report that Europeans keep in touch after they return home (compared to 52% of the Asians and 37% of the Latin Americans);
- 68% of the Africans see the Europeans working harder than themselves (compared to only 35% of the Asians and 37% of the Latin Americans);
- 80% of the Africans see it 'harmful' that Europeans put forward their views during meetings (compared to 56% of the Asians and only 33% of the Latin Americans);
- in the completed answers to the open questions we see that it is primarily Africans who talk about an annoy-

ing superiority complex of Europeans and their lack of understanding of the practical problems to realise something in Africa.

Asian respondents leap less to the eye – possibly because they themselves form a more mixed culture – when it comes to creating opinions:
- yet 74% of the Asian respondents suspect that it is acceptable for Europeans to object to their superiors (compared to 52% of the Africans and 50% of the South Americans);
- 'only' 48% of the Asians appreciate that Europeans come to the South on a mission to help the poor (compared to 72% of the Africans and 87% of the Latin Americans);
- 44% of the Asians consider it 'harmful' that Europeans expect that the other speak their language (compared to 24% of the Africans and 21% of the Latin Americans);
- the latter appears also through the answers to the open questions. A Chinese respondent suggests explicitly that Europeans must be able to speak the local language. Likewise, the terms 'arrogance' and 'lack of respect' appear – as is the case with the Africans – whenever one describes the Europeans.

Latin Americans appear somewhat positive in their judgement of the Europeans and estimate the differences between themselves and Europeans to be smaller:
- 75% of the Latin Americans say that Europeans want to know them personally (compared to 48% of the Africans and 43% of the Asians);

- 88% say that the Europeans take their time to listen to them (compared to, for example, 63% of the Africans);
- 88% assume that Europeans are interested in their culture (compared to only 44% of the Africans and 56% of the Asians);
- Moreover, considerably more Latin Americans than Africans and Asians find that European leaders do not delegate (33% compared to 11% and 13% respectively) and that a European executive must keep a visual contact with his subordinates (50% compared to 15% and 9% respectively);
- for their own country 54% of the Latin Americans find that women are considered for leadership (compared to 28% of the Africans and 26% of the Asians); 42% suggest that it is acceptable by them to object to a superior (compared to 11% of the Africans and 9% of the Asians);
- in the open questions the Latin Americans underline, more than the other respondents, the good experience that they have with Europeans and the differentiation between European nationalities.

Across the continents it seems that businessmen have a more positive view of Europeans: they come here well prepared (100% of the businessmen report) and they listen to us in meetings (92% report). NGO-people are more severe critics: 50% of them find Europeans not interested in their cultural identity (compared to 11% of the businessmen).

Female and male respondents show no significant differences in their opinion about women being considered for leadership in the South. However less female than male respondents express that it is different in Europe: only 65% of the female respondents think that it is equal for men and women in Europe with respect to leadership, compared to 81% of the male respondents.

Strangely enough the frequency of contact with Europeans had little to do with influencing perceptions. The only point where there are significant differences is around the statement 'They do not understand our way of speaking', with 50% of those with frequent contacts finding it 'harmful' (contrary to only 18% of those with infrequent contacts). We may thus surmise the view that one has about perception being certainly as important as real experiences. However perception as well as earlier experiences form a predisposition which one should take into account.

Image and reality

The survey, which is discussed above, has investigated the perceptions of professional people located in the South about their European business relationships. Perceptions find themselves in the continuum between image and experience, they have been themselves collectively measured, and are not per definition a representation of reality. On the other hand, perceptions shape a reality by themselves: often one positions one's self in front of another on the ground of the image that one has of the other and hence one deals as such. That is why it is important to register perceptions.

The survey confirmed amongst other things that people from the South have a different approach to time than Europeans, that they see Europeans separating business from the personal (which is less the case in the South) and that there are serious differences in the approach to (ascribed) leadership. One sees that Europeans appreciate advance planning more than own compatriots, they come faster to the point during a meeting, they take less time to learn to know each other and often one hears nothing from them after they have left. The latter is not greatly appreciated. It fits into the image that the South has of Europeans: 'they do their best for everything to go smoothly, they adapt their external appearances, but they are not really interested in our culture in depth. Apart from that, they dare to come out as dominant and they want us to accept their point of view instead of aiming towards a consensus'. With respect to leadership one observes that Europeans delegate easier and they have less need to exercise direct supervision. Women are more accepted in leadership roles and, that is how it is felt, it is much more acceptable to object to a superior in Europe that it is in the South.

The perceived differences between the South and Europe surface more explicitly in the opinions of the Africans. They feel more strongly than the others that Europeans come out as dominant. They themselves appear more particularistic, where personal ties are considered more important for professional cooperation. What is felt more than often as problematic in Africa is this presumed totally different attitude of Europeans in this area. Asians have a less philanthropical image of Europeans but they are equally irritated about the sort of superiority feeling that Europeans have. The most positive judgement of the Europeans come from our Latin American sample which also places itself closer to the Europeans than the Africans and the Asians.

These survey is based on a very small sample. One must not draw universal patterns out of it. It worth repeating such survey, spread over a much larger sampling population and targeting a specific profession in a specific country. Only in such a way one will one come closer to some sort of representation.

There are enough indications from this survey to find that the moment of the meeting, the 'intercultural momentum' is often the determining factor for further development of a partnership. The appeareance of Europeans, the respect for a different approach to time and the sincerety of their interest, are determining factors for the attitude of their partners in the South as much as the contents of their project and the advantages that they offer. Each meeting is a chance for a multiplying friendship, in the length of time and over a great number of people. To paraphrase Shakespeare, we can suggest: 'the good things that men (or women) do, live after them'.

In a nutshell the survey taught us that people in the South attach more importance to the intercultural momentum than Europeans do. An intercultural momentum must according to them become deeper, in the sense that one must take more time to listen to one another. Subsequently it must be cherished, personalised, take the form of more than a mere business relationship, to contain hospitality... It must also be stretched, in other words to be extrapolated to the future. And finally it offers the opportunity to generate mutual acknowledgement and equality between people of different cultures.

NOTES

1. After the cold war such searches into "the big cultural difference" or "the tensions that differences bring" were very popular amongst the circles of western academia and the opinion makers. See amongst others Barber B.J. (1996), *Jihad vs McWorld*, Ballantine, New York; Huntington S. (1996), *The clash of civilisations*, Simon & Schuster, New York; Inglehart R. & Carballo M. (1997), Does Latin America Exist? (And is there a Confucianist culture): A Global Analysis of Cross-Cultural Differences, *Political Science and Politics*, 30, no. 1: 34-47; Landes D. (1998), *The wealth and poverty of nations*, Norton, New York; Harrison L. & Huntington S.P. (eds.) (2000), *Culture matters – How values shape human progress*, Basic Books, New York.

2. In the meantime there has already been profound opposition against the ideological, 'ethnocentric' and above all the essentialistic approach which is at the bottom of many studies. What is above all fascinating is the increasing literature which contradicts itself by attacking the western cultural monologue from other cultural backgrounds. Examples are Maalouf A. (1998), *Les identités meurtrières*, Grasset & Fasquelle, Paris; Vale P. & Maseko S. (1998), South Africa and the African Renaissance, *International Affairs*, vol. 74, no.2 : 271-287 ; Sen A. (2005), *The Argumentative Indian – Writings on Indian history, culture and identity*, Picador, New York.

3. Hofstede G. & Hofstede G.J. (1991), *Cultures and Organisations: Software of the Mind. Intercultural Cooperation and Its Importance for Survival*, New York: McGraw-Hill, 1991.

4. Schwartz, S. & Sagiv L. (1995), Identifying Culture-Specifics in the Content and Structure of Values, *Journal of Cross Cultural Psychology*, no. 26, pp. 92-116.

5. 25 of these statements refer to the cultural meeting itself: the manner of announcements, the preparation, the time management, the way of negotiation, the mixture of the professional and the personal, hospitality, dealing with appearance norms, dedication and perception of reality; based on those points the respondents were asked to evaluate their own performance and that of their European partners (or Europeans in general). 13 additional statements refer to the conditions of experiencing this cultural meeting: work related perception of values. It is all about delegating or being able to delegate, the role of women, the importance and the indisputed character of leadership and authority, planning and adherence to the rules (*vs* improvisation) and the importance of regular contact. Here it is also asked to compare own perception of values with the perceived ones of the Europeans. Subsequently, the extent is investigated to which certain characteristics of Europeans (for example rushing matters, not showing any real interest, etc) can damage professional relationships. 10 characteristics are hence given in that manner. For a last batch of questions 7 possible motives of Europeans were given, with the request to choose to what extent this or that motive plays an important part (for example investing, a desire to help the poor, interest in the local culture, a sort of tourism,...). Open questions, linked to the prestructured ones, are asked about factors responsible for success or failure in intercultural partnerships, other attitudes worth mentioning which one perceives Europeans to have and their opinion about the questionnaire. At the end there are few personal characteristics to fill in: nationality, sex, age, profession and frequency of contact with Europeans.

6. Apart from obviously obtaining a first insight in the perceptions in the South on interculturality, the purpose of the survey was to test the validity of the questionnaire, whether it was user friendly and its discretion – and not about the number of respondents.

7. Parsons T. (1959), *The social system*, Free Press, New York

8. Trompenaars F. & Hampden-Turner C. (1993), *Riding the Waves of Culture*, McGraw-Hill, London.

9. Furthermore we must not forget that more than half of the respondents directly or indirectly are active in the development collaboration area.

THE AUTHORS

Prof. Dr. Ir. Koenraad Debackere is Chairman of the Living Stone Centre and General Manager of the K.U.Leuven (Catholic University of Leuven), Belgium

Prof. Dr. Patrick Develtere is the academic director of the Living Stone Centre and head of research group on sustainable development of HIVA (Higher Institute for Labour Studies), K.U.Leuven, Belgium

Bob Elsen is Managing Director of the Living Stone Centre and of Joker Toerisme NV (Mechelen, Belgium)

Ignace Pollet is senior researcher at HIVA (Higher Institute for Labour Studies), K.U.Leuven, Belgium